THE MILLION POUND
PROPERTY EXPERIMENT

BOOKS

This book is published to accompany the television series entitled *The Million Pound Property Experiment*, first broadcast on BBC2 in 2003.

Executive producer: Paul Wooding
Series producers: Jane Merkin and Ann Banks

Published by BBC Books, BBC Worldwide Limited, Woodlands, 80 Wood Lane, London W12 0TT

First published 2003
© Colin McAllister and Justin Ryan 2003
The moral right of the authors has been asserted.

ISBN 0 563 48813 1

Commissioning editors: Rachel Copus and Nicky Ross
Project editor: Sarah Miles
Copy-editor: Judith Scott
Designer: Isobel Gillan
Picture researcher: Frances Topp
Art director for jacket: Pene Parker
Production controllers: Belinda Rapley and Christopher Tinker

Set in Minion and Helvetica Neue
Colour separations by Radstock Reproductions Ltd, Midsomer Norton
Printed and bound in Italy by L.E.G.O. Spa

BBC Worldwide would like to thank the following for providing photographs and for permission to reproduce copyright material. While every effort has been made to trace and acknowledge copyright holders, we would like to apologize should there be any errors or omissions.
Business a.m. p4; Red Cover p8, p17; The *Guardian*/Don McPhee p15; Matthew Morgan p23, p26/27, p37, p46/47, p58, p75 above and below; getmapping.com p24/25; Michael Shanly Homes p31; Trip/H Rogers p43 left; Houses and Interiors p43 centre and right; IPC Syndication p71, p150; View/Peter Cook p73.
All other photographs by Robin Matthews © BBC Worldwide 2003.

Special thanks to A1 Garage Doors, Alan Higgs Architects, Anglian Windows, Associated Weavers Europe Ltd, Bradley Furniture, Carpets International (UK), Castle Integrated Systems, Classic Drapes by Erica, Collins and Hayes Ltd, Collinson Ceramics (Scotland) Ltd, där lighting ltd, Dorma, Gaskell Carpets Ltd, H J Contracts Ltd, Knoll International, Living Connections Ltd, Miele, Moods Bathrooms, Multiyork Furniture Ltd, Nono, Paint & Paper Library, Peter Walker Group Ltd, The Polished Floor Company Ltd, RMC Aggregates Ltd, Safestyle UK, Sanderson, Saniflo Ltd, Spratts, Suite Ideas, Taylor Walton, TKMaxx, Victoria Carpets Ltd, Vokèra Ltd and Wallace Sacks Lifestyle Ltd.

For my parents, Trudy and Robert, for giving me life and love, for Justin who shares it all with me, and for Felix and Winston. Love Colin.

For my late father, Dan, who I miss every day. Thank you, simply, for being. For my mother, Claire, for her constant support and love, for Carmel, Colette and Damian, for my two best boys Felix and Winston, and for Colin who puts up with me through thick and thin. Love Justin.

ACKNOWLEDGEMENTS

A huge thank you to Ann Banks for much valued friendship and comic timing, for steering the way and making it all such fun (we will *never* forget *that* boat trip); to Jane Merkin for subsequent navigation; to Kristian 'here come the bears' Digby and Adam Purver for seamless direction; and to Emily Rusted, Michelle Furey and Sophia Wollschlager for action well beyond the call of duty.

Special thanks to our very first 'renovator', Nigel Leck, who made us laugh through difficult times; to Andy Graham, Susan Stevens and Alan Higgs for guidance; and to the tradespeople who built our dreams.

Thanks to Caroline Feldon for diva sessions; to Ellena Stojanovic, Juliet Henson, Varsha Chauhan, Natasha Wood, Roddy McKinnon, Steve Peet, Tom Green, Paul Ward; and to all the camera and sound crews for capturing it all so beautifully.

Thanks to Jane Root, Ann Morrison and Tessa Finch for keeping the faith; to Alison Sharman and Jane Lush; to Sue Watson, Sharon Fisher and Katie Wright for seeing past 'the medicine cabinet'; to Amanda Lowe for *everything*; to Rosemary Edwards for fashion coordination; and to Maggie Davies and all at Pebble Mill.

Thanks to all at BBC Worldwide, especially Nicky Ross, Sarah Miles, Rachel Copus, Isobel Gillan, Robin Matthews, Frances Topp, Sarah Edgehill, Judith Scott, Tessa Clark and Margaret Cornell.

Thanks to Sue Knight at Knight Ayton Management for guiding our careers.

A big up to our Glasgow team – Debby McGregor, Natasha and Gordon Russell, John Amabile, Alyzen Thyne, Grahame McGowan, Fhiona Mackay, Peter Samson and Elaine and George Ponte; and to Kate McGhee and Heidi for looking after our homes in Scotland and Birmingham.

Thanks also to Beverly Brown for providing the first rung on our career ladder at SMG and to Cate Devine at the *Herald*, both of whom pointed us in the right direction; and to Eileen Easton, our editor at *Business a.m.*

Finally, thanks to Kelly Hoppen and Jasper Conran, both huge sources of inspiration, and to Jibby Beane for her joie de vivre!

CONTENTS

▲ Colin (left) and Justin have used their skills and experience to climb the property ladder themselves and now live in their own dream house in Glasgow.

Introduction

Many years ago, in a mystical and magical land called Scotland, two young boyz became absorbed by the wonderful world of interiors. Without any formal artistic education, they gained their knowledge via curiosity and a determined interest in all things that pertained to cool living. Neither of them studied design – Colin did business studies at Glasgow College of Commerce and Justin did psychology at Glasgow University – but their education meant Colin was able to hone his business skills while Justin learnt a little about what makes people tick. This education would come in *very* handy in later life …

When they were students in the mid-1980s, both lived variously in halls of residence and student flats and during that time they tried to make their homes thoroughly contemporary. The first thing Justin did on moving into his halls of residence room in Glasgow's West End was to colour-wash its institution-white walls with a soft salmon, before replacing the brown stripy curtains with single panels of terracotta fabric and the carpet with an offcut purchased from a local DIY store. Colin moved into his first student apartment and gutted the entire three-bedroomed space (much to the chagrin of his flatmates, who didn't have much say in the matter) over just one weekend. With the motto 'If it doesn't move, sponge it …' he worked his way from one end to the other with a myriad contrasting – sorry, make that clashing – shades that would have made Joseph's coat blush. But *sponging*? Well, back then it looked fabulous and everyone seemed to love what he did.

After leaving further education the boyz tried various jobs – in Colin's case, in local government interspersed with escapist evening jobs, including film extra, catwalk model and pop video dancer, and, in Justin's, in finance and theatre. OK, for *theatre* read working in a café at one of Glasgow's leading playhouses. But this wasn't where their true passions or talents lay.

Make-over madness

The turning point came when a local TV station approached the boyz to appear on a show to discuss the whys and the wherefores of home improvement. Allegedly skilled at transforming trash into treasure and the humdrum into the glamorous (they raided skips and plundered second-hand stores for design inspiration), they attracted the attention of local magazines, one of which invited them to turn an ancient Lloyd Loom chair into a funky gold and blue throne. *Hmmm.* Anyway, to cut a long story short, that one-off article became a monthly feature, which in turn led to a regular make-over slot on *Summer Discovery*, a magazine show on the Scottish ITV network.

They were soon merging property skills and home styling expertise on their own daytime series for the BBC, *Trading Up*, where they tackle the problems faced by home-owners up and down the country who are having difficulty selling their houses. *Real Rooms* and *Housecall* are two other series where they get to flex their design muscles, showing at the same time that successful home styling needn't cost the earth.

The first rung on the property ladder

Their steady climb up the property ladder was, in the beginning anyway, an unconscious thing. Moving around the rental sector, initially as students and latterly as young professionals, they soon realized that the rental game simply lined the pockets of the city's anonymous landlords. So they started looking at properties that would divert some of that income into their own bank accounts. A lucky move into a one-bedroom apartment – all they could afford at that time – saw a £25,000 first-time buy in the city centre soar to more than double that in the first 18 months. They invested perhaps £100 to reface the kitchen doors with timber laminate, and lavished approximately £200 on a budget carpet and another £100 on paint but that was about it. The rest was simply styling, a few key accessories and some clever lighting. They were off …

Selling that flat allowed them to buy their next property, a two-bedroom, newly built apartment, which at £43,000 was £7000 less than the one they had just sold but with an extra bedroom. Located half a mile from the buzzing city centre in an area known as Cathedral Precincts, the apartment was sold to them by a builder in collaboration with a housing association. Properties were being marketed either on the basis of shared ownership or a regular 100% purchase. The boyz chose the latter and so the subsequent profit was 100% theirs. They enjoyed a brand-new kitchen and bathroom, a huge living room and two bedrooms – not to mention manicured private grounds and parking – for just 18 months before selling on at a £16,000 profit. They did little to the place apart from moving in, adding carpets and furniture and then moving out a year and a half later. And they didn't plan to make a profit; they simply decided that they wanted to move back into the city centre proper. They wanted bars, clubs and restaurants on their doorstep without the half-mile walk from Cathedral Precincts.

And so it came to pass that they moved again. A £43,000 'repossession' apartment in College Lands (an old whisky bond) turned out, a year later, to be worth £62,000 after they had stamped their mark on it, yet, as on every previous occasion, there had been no premeditated attempt to make money. It just seemed that they had an innate ability to send property prices soaring. Next, the boyz spotted a sales board perched six floors up in a neighbouring block. Tempted by the prospect of city views (the College Lands apartment had looked directly onto uninspiring semi-derelict warehouses) they made an appointment to view the £45,000 flat. What they encountered surprised even them and should be a worthwhile lesson to anyone studying potential property details. What was described in the sales particulars as a run-down, two-bedroom flat was so much more – loads of space, huge picture windows, a dining terrace and a 25-foot balcony, not to mention a modern kitchen and a spacious bathroom. And what's more, due to the lacklustre sales brochure, no one else was looking. The downside? Some minor, easily repairable smoke damage (which made the place look far worse than it actually was) and a cracked window. Hooray! City living at its most glamorous, roof-top best was only a weekend of decorating and 50 yards of new carpet away. The costs were modest to say the least – a spend of £1500 covered the entire repair and redesign package and resulted in a £79,000 selling price just three years later. Result!

At-a-glance guide to our journey up the Glasgow property ladder

	LOCATION	BOUGHT FOR	COSTS	WORTH WHEN SOLD	YEAR BOUGHT IN	LIVED THERE FOR
1	City centre	£25,000	£400	£50,000	1988	18 months
2	Cathedral Precincts	£43,000	£500	£59,000	1990	18 months
3	College Lands	£43,000	£1000	£62,000	1991	2 years
4	Candleriggs	£45,000	£1500	£79,000	1993	3 years
5	West End	£75,000	£4000	£230,000	1996	7 years
6	Kelvingrove Park	£500,000	£200,000	estimated £1,000,000	2003	6 months so far

When they tired once more of the city centre they moved to the fabulously cool West End of Glasgow and into a red-sandstone seven-room flat. Tired, tatty and more than a little worn around the edges, it simply needed a little TLC to make it shine. At £75,000 it seemed like a reasonable buy, but was valued at £230,000 seven years later – they really had struck gold. Especially when you consider that they spent only £4000 on it overall – on some new kitchen cabinets, around 70 litres (15 gallons) of paint and 10 days of intensive floor sanding. Time to stay put? Well, actually, no. With the seven-year itch scratching furiously, the boyz spotted an incredible opportunity in Kelvingrove

Park, an area they'd always admired. Occupied by a Scottish shipping company, this was a large Victorian town house with massive potential. With one eye on nesting and another on investing, they found its charm irresistible. The last step on their own Million Pound Property Experiment? Only time will tell. It's been a long journey but they – sorry, *we* – have enjoyed every minute.

Why should you go upmarket?

You should go upmarket for one simple reason – *because you can*. Aspiration is healthy because it drives and pushes us to go that extra mile to achieve our goals. Life can be a long hard struggle and it's nice to think that there might be the odd stepping stone here and there to help us on our way.

In today's world you only have to turn on your television or pick up a newspaper and the term millionaire is never far away. We all dream of fast cars, second homes and luxurious holidays, but those who achieve these things are in the tiny minority. As a nation, however, we do now holiday abroad more, read more, eat out more and consequently, as we experience more, want even more. Prowl your own high street and observe how many stores now carry exclusive ranges like Gucci and Prada, labels that were once the reserve of the world's fashion capitals. Top scores for marketing on the part of those designer brands, but if there was no demand there would be no supply. Confidence and aspiration now seem to be part of the national ethic.

If this is to be your first step into the property arena stick with us, because we can help you become a real financial contender. But you're going to have to work for it. The main point that we make over and over again in this book is that you have to learn to understand your market. If you make the right decisions your earning potential will spiral to a level far beyond your wildest dreams. Every project you tackle will be different but you will always need to expect the unexpected. There are always going to be problems that you could not have foreseen, and sometimes you will get to a point where you'll wish you had never started. But be brave! We are here to guide you through every step of the process. The purpose of *The Million Pound Property Experiment* – the book and the TV series – is to try and inject some of our own experience into your life. We can't promise miracles but we can promise to give you our best impartial advice. Learn from our mistakes and gather strength from our successes. Your own success is just around the corner …

What we did before and during *The Million Pound Property Experiment* was simple: we just switched on to what makes property better and ultimately more valuable. For the price of a book we'll show you how to ensure financial security for your own future. Enjoy. Oh, and good luck!

What do you want?

Having established that there is some serious cash to be made from climbing the property ladder, the best way forward is to analyze what you really want. It's all very well proclaiming 'I want to make money' but unless you're entirely realistic from the start you will not achieve the optimum profit. However, if you deal with each property-buying project carefully from the outset you'll make substantial returns. Remember that buying a property is like any other investment: results aren't guaranteed and there will always be an element of risk. But if you study form (like you might with a racehorse, for example) you can often improve your chances of a profit quite substantially. To make a sensible investment you must always do your homework. It's certainly possible that you might just strike lucky and buy a hot property without knowing what you are doing, but you're just as likely to make an expensive mistake. Our best advice at this stage is to consider everything, get to know your potential marketplace inside out … and take nothing for granted.

▼ However far up the property ladder you hope to climb, having a clear idea of exactly what you want to achieve will make the journey a lot easier.

If necessary, you'll have to move to where you think opportunities are best, rather than the area you might choose yourself. However, if you *are* serious about investing to make a profit, rather than simply upping the value of your home by the cost of your invested labour, this shouldn't be a problem. It's simply a case of 'going where the money is' ...

Certainly, life can be *dramatically* improved by incremental property ascension, but even if the cash-in-hand element is not at the forefront of your mind there is still benefit in kind to be had from doing the same research and applying the same principles. Consider having a better home with more space, a generally better lifestyle and arriving in a better area as a result of consecutive non-lateral moves and you'll realize there is much to be gleaned within the chapters of this property bible.

Attitude to risk

- Risk is a major part of any investment, whether large or small. It's best to figure out how you feel about this before you put your foot on the first rung of the property ladder.
- Remember if you're buying to sell on, you will still be parting with monthly mortgage repayments while you own the property.

What sort of investor am I?

Property investors fall into three distinct categories: long term, medium term and short term. Which type are you?

Long-term investors expect to stay in their homes for many years and any improvements that they make to their property will tend to be determined purely by their own taste and needs. They do expect the value of their property to increase over time, of course, but profit *per se* is not their main concern.

Medium-term investors typically move house every two or three years and they will be looking to trade up, having made a substantial profit, each time. They are likely to renovate their property in line with prevailing tastes and fashions and will go for improvements that they know will be attractive to prospective buyers. These investors are interested in creating profit fairly quickly and tend to think in terms of climbing up the property ladder. They may well put market considerations before their own personal preferences.

Short-term investors are those who buy a property specifically in order to make money out of it as quickly as possible. These are the people who have turned property development into a business, so profitability is the key. They will avoid getting sentimental about any place they have bought and will always be ready to sell and move on.

Some investors may develop only two or three homes in a lifetime, while others may develop one or two properties a year. At the other end of the spectrum, serious speculators may have many projects on the go at one time. This last group represents the smallest proportion of investors, while the largest proportion falls into the first category. Following this book, however, will allow even those at the primary level of the property ladder to harness some of the skills of those who occupy the higher levels. Each case study will demonstrate how you can jump a little further ahead in the financial stakes.

Priorities

Having decided what kind of investor you are at the moment you need to decide whether you want to change. If you have a young family, for instance, would you want to move house every year while the children are growing up even though you realize that would be the quickest way to make a profit? And are you prepared to live in an almost permanent mess while you renovate each property you acquire, or to spend all your spare time working on it if you can't afford to give up your paid employment?

You need to consider why you are making a change. What are you planning to use the property for? How long are you planning to live there? You also need to think long and hard about what, exactly, you are trying to achieve. What is your ultimate property goal? Is it to live in a manor house in perfectly manicured grounds? Or to inhabit a glass-lined penthouse apartment in a cool part of town? Would you like to derive new income from a property investment that would allow you to replace your boring full-time job with a part-time vocational career? Or have you simply outgrown your current property?

Budget

From our own experience we know how easy it is to be seduced by the thought of what a property might look like after it has been renovated – indeed, our ability to see the potential in almost anything is one of our strengths. However, and it's a very big 'however', having vision and flair is not such an advantage when it means you get so carried away by a romantic notion that the budget goes out of the window. So do think the numbers through carefully before you start making serious plans.

The formula – how much will I make?

- Catapult yourself ahead to completion and establish an estimate of what your costs are likely to be. Budget for all associated expenditure such as estate agency costs, surveys and conveyancing, and generate a realistic idea of what your selling price will be by watching prices locally.
- Make sure you are well informed at every stage of the buying and selling process, and always allow a little bit extra in your budget to cover unexpected costs. With this in mind, take your purchase price, add in the cost of renovation plus all associated fees, deduct this total from your projected selling price – *et voilà* – there is your profit.
- Don't forget to take into account all monthly costs while the property remains unsold, including utilities (gas, electricity and water), mortgage repayments, insurance and council tax.

How to use this book

In this book we'll tell you how you can climb the property ladder by improving each property you buy in such a way as to maximize its value. Whether you need to tackle just one room in your home or whether you need a complete make-over, there is a section here that will show you how.

We'll identify the bonuses – and the pitfalls – of putting your hard-earned cash into bricks and mortar, and give you an overview of just how lucrative dealing in the British property market has been for some people in the last few years. Spend a little time with us and you too will learn how to make substantial returns. And what's more, you don't have to be based in London to chase those profits. As you will see from the real-life case studies, complete with breakdowns of timescales, costs, profits and details of all the changes made, there are plenty of opportunities out there in all parts of the UK.

In the first section of this book we take you carefully through the whole process of buying a new home. We'll help you find a property with potential, show you how to assess the marketplace, tell you all you need to know before you buy and explain the ins and outs of making an offer. In the second section we look at every aspect of your home, both indoors and out, and give advice and inspiration for both cosmetic and structural alterations. And when you finally get around to selling your property, the third section has all our advice on how to maximize your profits, including our trade secrets for 'staging' your home for your target buyer.

BUY

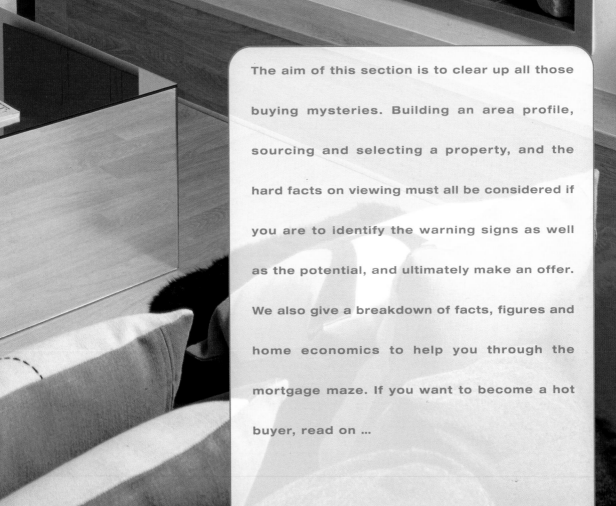

The aim of this section is to clear up all those buying mysteries. Building an area profile, sourcing and selecting a property, and the hard facts on viewing must all be considered if you are to identify the warning signs as well as the potential, and ultimately make an offer. We also give a breakdown of facts, figures and home economics to help you through the mortgage maze. If you want to become a hot buyer, read on ...

ING

Finance

We've all done it, haven't we? At some point we've thrown ourselves onto the sofa with a bottle of wine and a list of properties from the estate agent and gone on a fantasy journey. We've imagined ourselves in a stunning penthouse or on a wonderful country estate with the cares of the world behind us. And where's the harm in this? As far as we are concerned it's actually a good thing. While other advisers might suggest realism at all times, we're all for a bit of future planning – 'What the mind can conceive and believe, you can achieve.' Dreaming fires the heart and gets the imagination working, though good old reality does tend to bite in the end. But hey …

So what can I afford?

Before you start seriously looking for a property, work out what you can afford and what all the costs involved will be so that you don't overcommit yourself. Consider all your monthly outgoings and balance these against your income to work out your buying power. Be realistic. You may, for example, have to sacrifice a planned holiday or a new car. Are you prepared to do that? Also, think about ways of boosting your income, such as taking on a part-time job or letting out a room in your new property. Don't rely on this, though, because nothing is guaranteed and you need to ensure you can cover your costs.

What can I afford?

How much do you spend on:
- Current mortgage or rent?
- Utility bills (gas, electricity and water)?
- Entertainment and travel?
- Food?
- Car?
- Credit cards?
- Loan repayments?
- Insurance?

How much can I borrow?

As a general guide, most lenders will offer you a mortgage of three times your annual gross income, which means that if you earn £20,000 you should be able to borrow £60,000. Things are slightly different if you're buying with another person, because lenders adjust their figures accordingly and will

usually offer you around two and a half times your joint annual gross income. So if you earn £20,000 and your partner earns £10,000 you should be able to get a mortgage of around £75,000. There is another sort of package for couples, whereby the offer is based on the larger annual income multiplied by three, plus the smaller annual income counted once: so if you earn £20,000 and your partner earns £10,000 you'll be able to borrow £70,000. It's worth working out all the potential sums involved, because you'll usually find that two people can borrow more by using the traditional 'two and a half times' method.

Now prove it

Whichever way you work out the loan your lender will usually want proof of your earnings. This is easy enough if you've got an employer who can hand over official documentation, but if you're self-employed you may have to produce accounts going back three years. Having said that, there are specialist lenders who offer mortgages to people who don't fit the usual earning patterns, and nowadays a growing number of borrowers are declaring their

▼ It pays to shop around when looking for the best mortgage package. High-street banks, estate agents and specialist mortgage companies all offer a range of opportunities that can be tailored to suit your needs.

own income on mortgage application forms. This is known as self-certification; lenders may use other forms of credit assessment to make sure they're not taking too high a risk in lending the money, then charge the borrowers a slightly higher interest rate.

Don't bite off more than you can chew

There are many specialist lenders and a huge variety of different loans, and whatever your financial circumstances there should be someone out there willing to lend you money. This is good news but it comes at a price: while it's great to think you can borrow huge amounts to afford your dream property, remember that any loan has to be affordable. Your mortgage lender will calculate a loan on the basis of what they reckon you can afford, but it's up to you to mention anything else that may affect your financial circumstances, such as credit card debts and student loans.

There are lenders willing to offer mortgages based on a higher salary multiplier than normal, for instance up to four or even five times your salary. This means you can afford a grander pad, but your monthly repayments will also be much higher and you won't be left with much disposable income for anything else. It's easy to say ' Well, I won't go out much for the next year or so', but owning a property brings responsibilities that don't always wait for an opportune moment; think about what you'd do if you needed to pay for emergency repairs to the roof or if the shower broke and caused a flood. Think about your future security as well – if things went pear-shaped at work, would you be able to afford your repayments?

Stamp duty

As if all the other associated expenses of moving house weren't already bad enough, stamp duty is another cost – and a hefty one – which clobbers anyone venturing into the world of real estate. While some costs can be negotiated down, or avoided completely by shopping around, stamp duty is set in stone. It is a tax that has to be paid to the government, whether you like it or not. The only home buyers who escape its clutches are those who buy property worth less than £60,000. Spend one pound more than that and you'll land yourself with a 1% purchase bill. The only good news is that this rate applies however much you spend until you hit the quarter of a million pound mark. If you spend over £250,000 the stamp duty levied will be 3% of the entire purchase price, and if you spend over £500,000 the figure rises to 4%. Ensuring you stay within these boundaries (even if only by a pound) will save you literally thousands.

Deposits

You may find a lender who will offer you a 100% mortgage, but most will expect you to come up with a deposit of between 5% and 15% of the purchase price. If you can get a big loan it's tempting to rush in and buy now, rather than save up for a larger deposit, but this isn't a good move.

The lowdown on down payments

1 The bigger the deposit you can put down, the smaller your mortgage and the lower your monthly repayments will be.

2 The smaller your deposit, the higher the chances of getting out of your depth if things go wrong in the future. 'Negative equity' plagued home-owners in the late 1980s, when a property boom was followed by a massive collapse in prices. People who had been tempted to take out 100% mortgages suddenly found that as prices fell their homes were worth less than their loans, so they either couldn't afford to sell or were forced to sell at a loss, which often left them owing their lender thousands of pounds. If you put down as big a deposit as possible there's more leeway if the market collapses and prices fall.

▲ Don't forget stamp duty when working out your costs – if you spend more than £500,000 on a property, you'll have to pay 4% of your purchase price.

3 The higher your deposit, the lower your MIG or Mortgage Indemnity Guarantee. This is a one-off fee, paid when your loan is set up; it's basically an insurance policy, taken out by the lender, which guarantees that if you default on mortgage payments they will get their money back. The fee is approximately 8% of the cash amount between 75% of the asking price and the actual mortgage level payable. This sounds complicated, but it's actually quite simple to work out: if you buy a property for £200,000 and put down a deposit of £10,000, you're effectively borrowing £190,000. As such, 75% of the asking price is £150,000, and the amount borrowed is £190,000, so 8% of this £40,000 difference is £3200. One thing to remember with MIG, though, is that not every lender charges it and this is a competitive market, so it's worth shopping around. There's a chance your lender will be so keen to keep your business that they'll reduce the MIG if you're persistent. If you are charged a MIG fee, pay it off in one lump sum rather than having it added to the mortgage because you'll end up paying interest on that extra amount for up to 25 years, making it very expensive.

Conveyancing

The solicitor who oversees your house purchase will charge you a fee for his services, and this varies hugely depending on the size of the property you're buying and its location. The good news is that conveyancing has become so competitive recently that shopping around for the best quote should save you a fair bit. For even the smallest studio flat, though, you're not likely to see change from £300 for conveyancing, and that could easily double in big cities. When you're shopping around, remember to ask about extras: for instance, your solicitor will carry out a local authority search of the area on your behalf, and this will cost between about £80 and £200, depending on where you live. It is possible to go along to the local council and get this information yourself, but you need to know what you're looking for and you risk missing things that might be relevant, such as outstanding planning applications. Unless you're confident you know what's what, it's probably more sensible to leave the search to your solicitor. You'll also have to pay a Land Registry fee of 1% of the purchase price, so that's £100 if your home costs £100,000. Smaller 'miscellaneous' costs also add up: for instance, £40 on deeds' fees and £25 on telegraphic transfers. Remember that you'll be billed as you go along for some of these costs, such as the search, but the balance will be due on completion, so this is a bill you won't be able to pay off over the next few months. You should also be aware that if you put in offers on several properties you don't end up buying, your solicitor will be charging you for all the work carried out, however minimal. So keep tabs on how much you're spending, because it's frightening how quickly it can add up.

Building insurance

Everyone who owns a property should have both contents and building insurance – it's not illegal to be without it, but it's as stupid as driving a car without insurance. Building insurance covers the bricks and mortar, so if your home is flooded or destroyed by fire, or if you need other structural repairs, that's the policy that pays out. Your mortgage lender has a vested interest in your property until the loan is paid off, so they may make it a condition of the mortgage offer that you also take out building insurance, arranged through them. However, the premium is likely to be higher than if you shop around and find an insurer yourself, so don't go with the lender unless you have to. Even if it is a condition of your loan offer, remember that after a certain period, usually a year, you're free to change insurer. If you buy a flat in a managed block it could be the case that all the leaseholders are covered by a joint policy, but your solicitor should find this out for you during the conveyancing process.

Mortgage arrangement fees

These are often charged on fixed rate mortgages, and can range from £100 to £300. But there are many types of mortgage on which fees aren't charged, so if the loan that appeals to you is subject to a fee look around to see if you can find a similar one that isn't. It's also worth going back to the original lender and asking if they'll waive the arrangement fee.

Finding your way through the mortgage maze

The mortgage market is a more complicated place now than it has ever been. Gone are the days when the only lenders were banks or building societies. Now you can get a loan from an online lender or a specialist mortgage finance company – even supermarkets have set themselves up as big players in the financial world. There are dozens of different types of mortgage, and ways of paying them off, which is why it's important to get proper advice.

Independent financial advisors can recommend the best product to suit your needs and select it from the thousands of deals currently available. The key word here is 'independent'; you need to be aware that some financial advisors are in fact 'tied' agents, which means they're either employed directly by particular banks or insurance companies, or they'll earn commission on any of that company's products that they sell. Qualifications vary, depending on whether advisors specialize in investment, mortgages or pensions, so to find a truly independent advisor contact IFA Promotions on 0800 0853250, or via www.unbiased.co.uk. Independent financial advisors should offer a choice of fees or commission; fees range from £70 to £200 per hour, depending on where you live, and IFAs should disclose what commission they'll be earning on anything they sell you.

Mortgage advisors will be able to keep you up to date on what's happening in the mortgage market, including the best options for you, and like IFAs they can compare a wide variety of mortgage deals. They also work on a fee or commission basis, and tend to charge a percentage of the loan on completion of the mortgage, often between 1% and 2% of its value. Always try to negotiate, though, because you can save yourself hundreds of pounds if a broker reduces his fees.

The different types of mortgage

There's a lot of technical mortgage jargon, which sounds pretty daunting to the uninitiated. Once you've done some basic research it's all quite straightforward, but you need to get your head round a lot of information first. There's no substitute for the personal touch and many lenders are only too happy to talk you through your options, and won't charge you a penny for doing it. So make appointments with at least a couple of different lenders: they'll be keen to sell you their products, but will also explain the basics. Remember, though, that this is a constantly changing market – interest rates go up and down, new products appear on the market. Once you know what you want you can start hunting around for the best deal. IFAs will know what lenders are currently offering, and specialist publications such as *What Mortgage?* are useful once you know the basics. Another good source is the financial pages of the Sunday papers, which carry weekly updates on interest rates and different types of loans. There are two main types of loan: repayment and interest-only.

Repayment mortgage
A repayment mortgage is a bit like a large bank loan, whereby you repay the money in instalments along with the interest charged by the lender, so that by the end of the term, usually 25 years, you'll have paid off your mortgage. During the early years you'll mainly be paying interest charges, and over time

your monthly repayments will go towards paying off the capital. Lenders usually insist you take out a life insurance policy to cover the mortgage in the event of your death, which is particularly important if you have dependants. Repayment mortgages are good in that, provided you make all the payments, you're guaranteed to pay off the loan; they can also be taken out over varying periods of time, from 10 to 35 years. However, they're not portable, so you'd have to take out a new loan if you wanted to move.

Interest-only mortgage

With interest-only mortgages you pay only the interest on the loan, at the same time putting money into another type of savings plan, which will pay back the loan at the end of the agreed term. This savings plan could be an endowment, ISA or personal pension, the idea being that the money in it is invested by an insurance company on your behalf, growing into a nice little nest egg over the years. So at the end of the mortgage term there should be enough there to pay back the mortgage loan, as well as a bonus for yourself. Of course, nothing in life is this easy – share prices can go up as well as down – so many of these investments haven't done as well as expected, and people who took out endowment policies years ago are now having to make up the shortfall themselves when there's not enough to pay off the loan after 25 years. However, an interest-only mortgage is relatively flexible, because you can often increase your savings to pay it off more quickly, or pay off some of the capital as and when you want during the term.

Interest rates

The interest on both types of mortgage can be charged in a number of different ways. Variable interest means that when the interest rate changes your payments go up or down accordingly; a capped rate means that there's an upper limit to which your interest rate can rise, so even if the lender's rate rises to 8%, if your mortgage is capped at 7% you pay no more than that. Fixed rate mortgages offer you a specified rate for a set period of time, say 6% for two years; even if interest rates change during that period you still pay 6% until the end of the two years, when you'll usually revert to a variable rate deal. This can be a gamble, because although it's great if rates go up, if they fall you'll end up paying over the odds. However, the benefit of fixed rate mortgages is that you know exactly how much you'll be paying for a set period, so there are no hidden surprises. Be aware, though, that many lenders charge fees for arranging fixed rate mortgages, and you could be charged a redemption penalty if you try to get out of the deal early.

Cutting your mortgage costs

1 Be aware that the way lenders charge interest can affect how much you pay. If they charge annually and in arrears this doesn't take acccount of repayments made during the previous 12 months. All the money you've paid to them during the previous year has been sitting in *their* coffers, but they don't give *you* credit for it, or set it against your loan, until annual calculations are made on the first day of the next year. However, if interest is calculated daily the debt is adjusted every 24 hours, taking every new payment into account, which makes a big difference in cutting the overall interest you pay.

2 Another important factor is the term of the mortgage. You don't have to stick to the standard 25-year period; if you want to pay slightly higher monthly premiums you can take out a 20-year or even a 15-year mortgage, which means you'll pay less interest in the long run.

3 A flexible mortgage works a little bit like a repayment mortgage. Basically it gives you the chance to repay more quickly, so is a good option if you think your earnings might increase dramatically in the future or if you might come into some money. You can pay in extra lump sums, whenever it suits you, so the overall amount of the loan reduces more quickly. You can also pay on a flexible basis, say 10 payments a year instead of 12, and even take a break from regular repayments if money is tight.

Summary guide to all costs

On a property costing £100,000, with a mortgage of £90,000, expect to pay:

Mortgage arrangement fees	£200 (lender may not charge)
MIG (Mortgage Indemnity Guarantee)	£1200
Financial advisor/mortgage broker	£200
Building insurance	£250
Valuation report (see page 45)	£150
Full structural survey (see page 46)	£600
Stamp duty (@ 1%)	£1000
Conveyancing fees	£450
Local authority search	£150
Land Registry	£100
Miscellaneous conveyancing costs	£75
TOTAL	£4375

How to build an area profile

If you invest in property with promise in a good area (or in an area that has potential to develop) you've already won half the battle. However, if you buy a property with promise in the *wrong* area you are asking for trouble. It really is absolutely vital that you know how to spot potential and you must, of course, take into account three other important factors: location, location and location. To make sound judgements about property you have to use your eyes, your ears and your feet. Go walkabout to establish a street-by-street profile of your target area and ask yourself what type of person lives – or, more importantly, would *want* to live – there. We call this sort of area-profiling 'eagle-eyeing' and it means that you are building up a picture in your mind of what a place is like.

Shops aren't just for shopping

One of our favourite ways to identify an up-and-coming area is to speak to the site-development departments at stores such as Marks & Spencer or Sainsbury's to find out where they are planning to open new shops. The same applies if they have already opened a store in your chosen area (see Case Study 1 on page 50).

These retail giants spend an awful lot of time and money working out whether a new area will be profitable for them, so why not hitch a ride on their expertise?

▼ Identify the demographic appeal of the area – does it suit the requirements of you or your potential market?

Five ways to find a property hot spot

1 Be aware of 'vehicular demographics' – or, in layman's terms, make a note of the types of car you can see parked in the area. Expensive cars equal expensive and desirable properties. Abandoned, vandalized cars spell trouble.

2 Look at how well the properties and their gardens are maintained. Pay particular attention to signs of an up-and-coming area, such as skips, recently cleaned buildings and evidence of developers converting large houses into smart new flats. Watch out, also, for changes in amenities – new bars, restaurants and shops are good signs, as are new transport links or anything that suggests continued investment in the area.

3 Find out who lives there. Young professionals? Families? Visit the area in the early evening to see who's coming home. Don't be afraid to take a sly peek through people's front windows when their lights are turned on. We're not suggesting you trespass on anyone's property, but a casual glance as you stroll by will do no harm and nosiness can pay big dividends!

4 Visit the local library and read as many back issues of the local newspapers as you can, especially the property pages, to build up a picture of the area. How are things changing? Are the amenities getting better or worse? Have some places ever been flooded? Has the crime rate improved? Check out the property prices. Do they seem to be going up more quickly in some areas than in others?

5 Visit the local council planning department to see whether there are any plans for the area that could affect property prices in the future. You may discover a road-widening scheme or plans for a new office block. Don't make the mistake of thinking that all development is automatically a bad thing: roadworks in one place could make the streets safer and quieter elsewhere, and companies moving into an area could mean that the people they employ will be looking for somewhere nearby to live.

▶ Before you begin looking for a property, it's vital to familiarize yourself with the area. Parks, schools, shops and good transport links are all signs of an attractive area in which to live or invest.

Potentially problematic properties

1 A property that is not convenient for local transport links and other amenities, such as shops, schools or recreational facilities.

2 A family home in an area with excellent schools and other facilities for children, but with no garden or one that is unsuitable.

3 A property that's been flooded in the past. Many people won't want to take the risk of flooding in the future and there may be problems getting insurance.

4 Anything on a busy flight path. Imagine the scene: you've done all that work, spent a fortune on repairs and your viewers have just arrived – at precisely the same moment as half a dozen 747s are circling overhead. *Quite.*

Marketplace anomalies

Each area will have a preferred house 'type'. It may be that some properties stick on the market for a long time because of an obvious 'blip'. Don't be put off by 'blips', as there could easily be a way to turn them to your advantage and make them work better with the area. Is that seemingly perfect house still on the market because it is a bedroom or two short of the 'ideal' in that particular area? Does it, on the other hand, have a large enough garden that could be converted to meet that demand? And how about parking? Is it good everywhere else except outside the property? It might be worth speaking to the local council about having the pavement 'dropped' so that you can pull a car into what is currently a small front garden. Success is often just a step away …

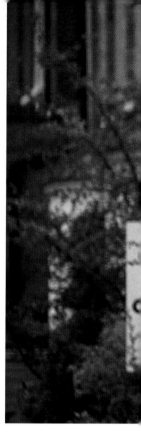

Property sources

For far too long estate agents and solicitors have cleaned up when it comes to selling property, but as the market expands so too are the avenues for buying and selling. While word of mouth and personal contacts might still be the way some houses are sold – there are properties at the top end of the market that are never advertised – the majority will be marketed *somewhere*. Leave absolutely no stone unturned in your search for the perfect property; the more ground you cover, the greater your chance of unearthing something really special.

Estate agents

Even with all the new marketing opportunities available, estate agents will probably still be your first port of call when you start looking for a property. Register your interest with every single local estate agency and then chase them up regularly to make sure they remember you and your requirements. And always let them know that you are a serious buyer and not a time-waster. Be clear about what you are looking for and how much you are prepared to spend, and make sure you have got your finances sorted out.

▲ Remember, estate agents don't only sell houses – they are also potential sources of valuable information. The more properties you look at and learn about, the better informed you'll be regarding prices in your area.

Doing the groundwork

Take a drive or walk round your area, look for sale boards and posters, and jot down contact details for reference. If a house has been on the market for a while the agent may have lost interest in it and forgotten to mention it to you.

Be eagle-eyed. Signs occasionally fall over, so look behind hedges as you scout around – perhaps last month's storms have toppled a sale flag and as a result fewer people are calling the selling agent for details. Fewer viewers mean fewer bids, which might in turn mean a lower final sale price – who knows?

The national press

As home interest and lifestyle magazines flourish (due in part to programmes like ours), so too do the property sections in the newspapers. These supplements make fascinating reading and usually include hundreds of advertisements placed by private sellers as well as estate agents. In London, for example, it's the *Standard* while in Glasgow it's the *Herald* and in Birmingham the *Post*. Supply and demand can fluctuate and there are new properties coming onto the market all the time, so it really is a case of checking the press *every* day so that you don't miss that ideal property.

How to be a 'hot buyer'

- When you visit or call an estate agent for the first time be clear about what you are looking for and impress them with how organized and focused you are.
- Tell the estate agent that you have already arranged your mortgage.
- Phone them back the next day to remind them who you are and to check they've got all your details.
- Learn the name of the person you are dealing with and start to build a relationship with them.

Internet

Most estate agents use the internet to promote themselves but there are also several specialist sites designed specifically for the property market. Choose a search engine like Dogpile or Ask, as these are compilation sites that utilize many other search engines as they explore the web. Use keywords, such as 'property in Birmingham' (or wherever you're looking), 'property for sale' or 'property in need of renovation' and see what comes up. Also think of searching in areas like 'businesses for sale', as it could be that your dream cottage is currently a newsagent that is ripe for conversion.

Many estate agents offer virtual tours on their websites – these provide a chance to look at a property, room by room, and give you a feel for the layout of the building. Of course, nothing beats getting out there and seeing the property at first hand, but it's useful to be able to whittle down the options and save time. We predict that the internet is a medium that will become more and more central to the buying and selling of property in the future.

How to research empty property

- Post a letter through the front door of the empty property, explaining your interest and asking the owner to contact you directly.
- Speak to the neighbours to find out who the owners are and where they can be found.
- Ask local estate agents whether they've been approached to sell the property.
- Play Miss Marple – visit the local library or council offices and check the electoral roll.
- Visit the property early in the morning and ask the postman if he knows the whereabouts of the owners – they could be having their mail redirected.

Auctions

Now this is a strange one as far as we are concerned. Previously the domain of properties that simply *couldn't* be sold, auctions have changed a little in recent times. In simple terms, an auction is a free-for-all where everyone sees what everyone else is prepared to pay. In many respects it provides the best forum for achieving the optimum price, particularly from a buyer's perspective. Its nearest 'relative', the sealed bids scenario set by an estate agent with a closing date for best and final offers, does not afford the luxury of knowing what other people's bids are, and therefore no last-minute chance to 'up' your bid if you really want the property.

If your auction bid is successful, you will have to put down a deposit – normally 10% – with the remainder due when contracts exchange. A particular drawback is that you must satisfy yourself that everything is structurally satisfactory before bidding starts. In short, you need to survey before the hammer starts to hover above your preferred lot.

And if your bid is unsuccessful? Well, you'll kiss goodbye to the survey fee for the property concerned. Lose out a few times and the costs could run into the thousands. You have been warned …

Auction advice

1 Do your research before the auction and get a survey done. Once your bid
has been accepted you will be fully committed.

2 Don't be misled by the auctioneer's guide price. If two or more bidders
really want a property the sky's the limit. We once saw a two-bedroom flat
in a Leeds suburb sell at auction for just under £100,000 when the guide
price was set at £65,000. It so happened that several interested buyers
locked horns and the price just went on spiralling upwards.

3 Decide in advance on the price you are prepared to pay and stick to it.
Don't get carried away or you will be financially embarrassed.

4 Don't be afraid to approach an auction house to make a bid in advance of the
sale. If the auctioneer conveys your interest to the owner they could accept
your offer on the grounds that a bird in the hand is worth two in the bush.
Failure to consider an early bid could result in the seller being left with an
unsold property if no one else puts their hand up on the big day.

Repossessed houses

There's no need to steer clear of properties that have been repossessed by a
mortgage company, as they can prove to be extremely lucrative purchases.
Repossessed homes are often sold for less than the market price, mainly
because they tend to be left in poor condition, often with their more valuable
assets, such as fitted kitchens or heating systems, removed.

Any perceived 'vulture' notions you may have can be redeemed by the
fact that you could actually be doing the debtor a favour. By buying their
property you could provide closure to an unpleasant period for them, and
they may be able to go some way to settling their outstanding debts and
getting back on track with their lives.

The early bird ...

One way of buying to speculate is known as the 'early bird option'. This is a
phrase coined by the house-building community years back and is now more
commonly referred to as 'buying off-plan'. An acquaintance of ours in
Scotland does this with any new developments that take her fancy. She only
has to see a sales cabin popping up on a new building site and she flies in for

further information. After she's done a spot of area-profiling of her own – and if she likes what she sees – she'll make an offer for one of the houses or flats in its unbuilt state. She'll buy at the first release price (usually substantially lower than subsequently released homes) and she'll sell when the site is complete. Her best deal to date is a three-bedroom villa located on the outskirts of Manchester, which she bought off-plan for around £110,000. She waited just short of six months, until all the neighbouring houses had been sold, and then put hers on the market. And the price? Oh, you know, nearly £150,000 – that's £40,000 profit. What's more, she only paid a 10% holding deposit to the developer, when she agreed to buy the house, and she didn't have to hand over the remaining 90% until the building was finished. Nice work if you can get it!

Be realistic

While all the aforementioned points are fairly general, they should provide a good basis for investigative research when your property hunt begins. On the negative side (and it'll do you good to step into that territory from time to time) remember that if a property deal sounds simply too good to be true it probably is. Always be on the lookout for the catch. That's not to say that there aren't many fabulous opportunities to be pursued (*The Million Pound Property Experiment* proves, of course, that there certainly are) but today the really good ones are thinner on the ground as more and more people muscle in on the property-development game.

Buying privately

From our own experience we have found that the people who sell their properties privately are confident that they can get a good price without using an estate agent. These people usually know what they are doing so you're unlikely to find many real bargains here. On the other hand, if the vendor wants a quick sale, they may be prepared to consider a sensible offer. After all, they will not be paying the usual estate agent's commission. So keep an eye out for private-sale boards and the small ads in the press. Bear in mind also that a search on the internet could pay off, as advertising newspapers such as *Loot* (www.loot.com), *Exchange & Mart* (www.exchangeandmart.co.uk) and *AdTrader* (www.adtrader.co.uk) also carry property sections. You might just find what you're looking for online.

Cold-calling

While cold-calling might sound an unlikely way to find the perfect property it shouldn't be discounted. It can, in fact, sometimes lead to some wonderful opportunities. Many of life's 'deals' are struck by simply asking questions. 'I'd like to buy a such-and-such – do you have anything available?' or 'I wonder if you can help me – I'm looking for a so-and-so.' As the saying goes, 'If you don't ask you don't get', so be prepared to give it a go.

While many of us might feel uncomfortable about knocking on the door of every property we fancy, most of us would be prepared to organize an inexpensive mailshot telling people what we're looking for. The wording can be as simple as 'Buyer seeks three-bed property in this area – any condition considered. No chain. Cash waiting. Please telephone blah blah blah …' It needn't be expensive either: a run of several thousand black-and-white fliers will only cost around £100, so it's a worthwhile investment. If there's someone out there who wants to sell discreetly, and without using an estate agent, you might just strike lucky.

We once sent the same letter to around 500 people asking if they were thinking of selling and suggesting that they contact us. Only four people responded; three of them were just curious to see if we would pay over the odds for their property, but the fourth enquiry came from a couple who were genuinely interested in meeting us and doing a deal – it so happened that they were thinking of selling their large apartment in Glasgow's West End when they saw our leaflet. We agreed a price and took possession approximately 10 weeks later. They were thrilled that it all went through so quickly and smoothly without an estate agent and we were happy with our new property and lived there for seven years.

▲ If you see signs of a new property development in your chosen area, make enquiries early on. Buying off-plan can be significantly cheaper than buying upon completion.

Relocation agents

While we were filming for *The Million Pound Property Experiment* in Harrogate we ran into an amazing woman who runs a relocation agency. She is not an estate agent herself, though she does work closely with them, but she certainly knows as much as they do about property, if not more. You could call her a private property detective. What she does is track down the ideal home for her clients and these people are hiring her for her time, her networking skills and her expertise in spotting an elusive property bargain.

A relocation agent will charge either a flat fee or a percentage (usually 1% or 2%) of the buying price, so, to be honest, it is a service geared towards the more affluent end of the buying market or those who are being relocated at the expense of their employers.

Letting agents

Another good way of finding out about properties that are not generally advertised is to talk to letting and rental agents. Not all landlords are interested in the rental market longterm, and many keep a stock of properties that they rent out while waiting for the market to change. So they might be persuaded to sell if prices are rising or they are not getting the rents they need. You may get a bargain if the landlord doesn't want the bother of renovating a property that has seen a succession of less than careful tenants.

Property managers

We are now going to tell you about one of our hitherto 'secret' ways of tracking down a good investment. The key is to establish a good relationship with the property managers or, as we call them in Scotland, 'factors', in your area. These people deal with properties that will never be seen in an estate agent's window and they have a hotline to landlords who may want to go for a quick private sale. Again, the accommodation will be in ex-rental condition, so you may be able to snap it up at a competitive price.

A friend of ours in Newcastle recently tracked down a three-bedroom terraced villa for an incredible £41,000 via a property manager. Sure, it needed redecoration throughout, not to mention a completely new bathroom and kitchen, but it had recently been rewired and replumbed. Anyway, around £4000-worth of DIY later, our friend had a cleverly redesigned house that was valued at £75,000. She decided to rent it out and accepted an offer of nearly £700 a month. The mortgage on the house means she is repaying around £300 a month, so her profit at the moment – before tax and expenses – is

£400 a month. So she is making nearly £5000 a year in rental income on a property that is appreciating nicely as Newcastle continues to get hipper and hipper. The bargains are there, if you can find them …

Freehold and leasehold

When you buy not just a property but also the land it sits on this is called 'freehold' and most houses fall into this category. It's the ideal way to purchase property, because the buyer owns everything and does not have to pay ground rent to a leaseholder. When a property sits on land owned by somebody else it is referred to as 'leasehold' and, in this case, the buyer has it for the duration of the lease only – after which the owner can reclaim his land, and consequently your property. This arrangement is common in blocks of flats and houses that have been subdivided. Remember that in Scotland some property laws are different to those in the rest of the UK and all residential property is freehold.

Leasehold properties are really only a good buy if they have a long lease, because this means you'll be able to sell on easily. Generally speaking, it's not ideal to buy a property with less than 50 years left on the lease as you could be paying a lot of money for something you may have to hand back at the end of that period. However, leasehold terms are no longer set in stone and the Leasehold Reform, Housing and Urban Development Act of 1993 allows joint leaseholders the opportunity to buy their freehold collectively. It also gives property owners a chance to extend their leases by up to 90 years.

Change of use

Bear in mind that you may come across – as we have done – some properties that require change of use certification. Residential opportunities can exist in offices, shops, hotels or public houses, to name but a few. Think about the style of each property rather than its current, or previous, use.

In our home town of Glasgow the buying of vacant ground-floor shops for conversion into modern housing stock has become very popular. In circumstances such as these it will be necessary to apply for change of use certification permitting a change from commercial to residential use, as well as satisfying any building consents or planning warrants for conversion works undertaken. Before pursuing your property dream, visit your local planning office and simply ask for advice. That, after all, is what they are there for.

The viewing

The most important part of buying a property is probably the initial viewing. This is when you are potentially at your most vulnerable, a time when you're likely to get carried away. It's all too easy to be so impressed with a property's few good points that you completely overlook its many serious drawbacks. If you are going to succeed at this game you will need to be cool and dispassionate.

The most important thing to remember is your frame of mind. Be decisive about what you're looking for and stay focused. And be cautious – your instinct may tell you you've found your dream property, but does it really suit your purpose? Make a list of your wants and needs for the property, whether you're buying for yourself and your family or want to develop and sell on, and keep it in the forefront of your mind. Look beyond what you see and try to find the potential in the place. What are you planning to do with it? Is there space for that extra bedroom you need? Most importantly, can you make these changes within your budget?

The very first time we invested in a property we were successful without even trying. We were not thinking about making a profit at the time, at least not our own – we just wanted to put a stop to landlords making a profit out of us as they had always done when we were students. So we bought the very first flat we looked at because it was the only one we could afford. It just happened to be in the right block, in the right street, at the right time, and because it was

Listed buildings

A listed property usually means the building has some interest, either historically or architecturally, and this can be very appealing to prospective buyers who want somewhere with character and history. Listed properties come in three different categories:

- Grade 1 – buildings of national interest, mostly public buildings and churches
- Grade 2* – buildings of outstanding interest, but in a more local context
- Grade 2 – buildings of special interest to be maintained and preserved

On the negative side, listed buildings are subject to strict planning regulations and consent may sometimes be withheld for structural or even cosmetic alterations. Conservation work can also be more expensive than standard building work – due to the specialist nature of the tasks involved and the building mediums required – so check what works need to be undertaken in the property, and cost them realistically before work commences.

in need of modernization and a little bit of TLC we decided to do it up. Within a year our £25,000 no-hoper that had been rejected by everyone else was a 'des res' worth £50,000. All we did was redecorate, lay new carpets and accessorize imaginatively. A mini property boom in Glasgow did the rest. We know how lucky we were. Home-buying for profit is becoming more of a science nowadays and one wrong purchase can spell disaster.

While we were filming *The Million Pound Property Experiment* we saw so many properties that we found it difficult to remember which was which. One two-bedroom apartment merged into another and each mid-terraced villa seemed exactly the same as the one before. We soon realized that we would need to stick to a few simple rules when viewing.

Points to remember

So what can you do to sort the wheat from the chaff when you're viewing property? You know how easy it is to forget exactly what a place is like as soon as you've walked out of the door, so take pictures and jot down your impressions while you're looking round. Then, as soon as you get home, make a list of all the pros and cons. Bear in mind what you've found out about the area. All things considered, have you ended up with more pluses than minuses? Picture yourself *in* the property – can you see your life going on in there? If the answer is no, don't adjust your lifestyle. Look for a different property.

Take pictures

What you see and what you remember about a property are often two different things, so it's a good idea to take photographs when you're viewing. Most people go for Polaroids to give them an instant record of everything they see, though this can get a bit expensive if you need to take a lot of pictures. Our record for viewings in one buying period is a scary 114, so we know how the costs can mount up. If you have a computer at home you would probably prefer to take pictures with an inexpensive digital camera and download them. If you have access to a home-video camera it makes sense to take it along to each viewing, so you can leave not only with visual documentation but also with a running commentary to help further, even if it's only to identify each room. If the owner is present ask their permission first – you don't want to offend them with comments about their home even if, to you, it's just information.

▲ Snapshots will remind you of the properties you view.

Use a notepad

Pictures will remind you of what the rooms in a property look like, but it's also useful to take notes while you are walking round. Use your notepad to record the observations your camera didn't capture. Was there a noise problem? What about parking outside? Did the property smell damp? Did the rooms feel cramped or gloomy? Did you talk to the neighbours? What did they say about the area?

Viewing both accompanied and unaccompanied

Your first viewing of a property will usually be in the company of the estate agent or the vendor. However, if you can persuade them to let you look around on your own on a subsequent visit you can set your own pace and give the place a much more thorough examination. If you're by yourself there'll be nobody trying to distract you from a property's poor features, and you won't be embarrassed about your reactions to another person's taste in decoration and furnishings. But whether you are unaccompanied or not assume nothing – remember, to assume makes an ASS of U and ME if things go pear-shaped at a later stage. So open all the cupboards and drawers and lift (without causing damage) any unfixed carpets. Poke about and check, check, check, for damp, for rot and all the other problems that might come back to haunt you.

Take your time, and ask questions

One thing to remember when viewing properties is not to rush. Give yourself plenty of time between appointments and look at everything in detail. Follow your instincts – if something doesn't feel right, ask yourself why and then quiz the estate agent and the vendors. (Vendors may be less guarded than their agents in what they tell you about themselves and their homes.) Ten minutes with your Miss Marple hat on could save you time and money. You need to know about every aspect of the property. How long has it been on the market? How many people have been to see it? Is there any flexibility on price? Have the owners made any changes to the property? Are there any problems that could affect future saleability, such as risk of flooding, subsidence or even difficult neighbours, etc? In any case, don't panic if you forget to ask all your questions: you should try to go back to a property a second or even a third or fourth time before you come to a decision about it.

Vital viewing questions

- Why are the owners moving?
- Are there any outstanding repairs to the property?
- What caused that crack/damp patch/hole, and is it getting worse?
- Do the owners have documentary evidence of all works carried out?
- What are the neighbours like?
- What's the parking situation like?
- Do the owners know of any building work planned nearby?
- What is the council tax banding? (Remember to enquire about heating costs and other amenities such as water and gas, as well.)
- Have the owners already bought another property? (This will help you ascertain how keen they are to sell.)
- Are the owners in receipt of any offers?

Divine inspiration – converting an abandoned church

One thing we considered doing while we were planning the television series for *The Million Pound Property Experiment* was to convert a beautiful deconsecrated hillside church in Malvern. The asking price was around £40,000 and we thought the building could be developed into four stunning executive apartments. Unfortunately, we were not able to pursue that particular opportunity at the time but we later found out that the church was indeed converted – precisely as we'd predicted – into four awesome homes. And the selling price? Oh, you know – only £250,000 each, which effectively creates a million-pound property! And the costs of conversion? Well, we can't answer that one with any real certainty as we didn't do the work, but we would expect – had *we* been on board – that costs would have been around £250,000 in total. We make that over £700,000 profit before tax. *Kerching!* This project would have been a massive undertaking, involving careful planning and months of hard work … But think of the returns …

The neighbours

Neighbours can be an invaluable source of information about a property and its environment, and it's always worth finding the time to talk to them. If you are looking at a flat don't forget to speak to the people immediately above and below it as well as those on the same floor. Ask them if they have any problems with the property and whether they are happy living there. Just as you quizzed the sellers, also enquire of the neighbours whether they know of any outstanding repairs to the building and about communal attitudes to paying for said repairs. And don't forget to ask if the block is a quiet place to live. Talking to neighbours may reveal nuggets of information that could help sway your buying decision, but remember that they won't automatically tell you everything, as they themselves may be thinking of selling and might prefer to keep certain problems concealed.

Some years back we were looking at a flat in a Victorian apartment block. We got talking to the people next door and they told us they themselves were thinking of selling. We ended up buying their flat for a considerably lower price than that of the flat we had originally come to view.

Five danger signs to watch out for

We would always recommend that you have a survey done on any property you intend to buy, but there are lots of things you can spot for yourself during a first viewing. If you know what to look out for, you could decide to walk away from a property before going to the expense of getting a surveyor in. On the other hand, if you can tell a vendor or an agent that you have identified a number of problem areas you will have put yourself in a strong position to get the asking price down. If you do find some of the obvious faults listed here it's up to you to decide, with the guidance of an expert perhaps, whether you can afford to deal with them and put things right.

1 Cracks – look for cracks in the plasterwork (interior) or masonry (exterior): the larger they are, the more worried you should feel. Both old and new plasterwork will tend to 'settle' on the surface of a wall or ceiling, causing hairline veining as a result of reacting to variations in temperature. Most of the time these tiny fissures are harmless and can be filled in and painted over. Deep cracks and those that seem to be getting worse in either stone or brickwork, however, should really set the alarm bells ringing as they could be symptoms of serious underlying structural problems. Underpinning a house is no picnic, so always get the advice of a surveyor or structural engineer in these cases.

2 Badly fitting doors and windows – watch out for any doors or windows that jam, stick or won't open and close easily. Do they appear to be out of alignment with their frames? If so, this could mean serious 'shift' or subsidence. Sometimes a crooked lintel or wonky door jamb is historical and non-progressive, meaning that the movement happened some time ago and isn't getting any worse. A survey will set your mind at rest and, again, if the problem is confirmed, you could still decide to go ahead and do the repairs.

3 Wet rot – while badly sealed window frames and deteriorated pointing might not sound like big issues there can actually be serious associated problems. If water has been allowed to seep into the space between window frames and brickwork this can spell ultimate disaster. What actually happens is that wet timbers eventually become wet rotten timbers, and as affected wood dries out it runs the risk of becoming dry rot (see below). Watch out for any evidence of this, and if the property looks and smells damp start asking why. Most problems with damp can be cured, though some remedies will be costly. Fixing a broken gutter and replacing a roof tile or window-frame joist will be quick and easy, but damp-proofing a basement with silicone and chemical injections or tanking it by stripping away all the affected areas, lining it with a waterproof membrane and then rebuilding the whole area would be a major expense.

4 Dry rot – this is a really serious problem in any property and until you know what to look for you won't necessarily spot it. Over the years we've learned to identify it by its distinctive smell. If you see any woodwork and timber that looks and feels crumbly or, even worse, has turned powdery, call in the experts. Dry rot can be much more difficult to isolate and eradicate than wet or damp rot and it does need to be treated thoroughly by professionals to stop it coming back. If it is left to develop unchecked the affected parts of a building will eventually start to fall down.

5 Wiring – use your eyes when checking out the electrics in a potential property. Are the plug sockets old and cracked? Do the metre and fuse boxes look like relics from Frankenstein's laboratory? Are there cables trailing everywhere because there's only one socket in each room? All these issues mean a rewiring job, which can, of course, be costly. Not only will you require the services of an electrician, but you'll also need a builder to dig out the wall channels for the new wiring and a plasterer to hide the damage. All this could potentially be a huge expense, especially when you consider that you haven't yet picked up a paintbrush. So do think before you act.

> ### Above and below
>
> If you're planning to commandeer the space underneath a ground-floor flat or the space under the roof above a top-floor one, in order to extend the property, remember to check the title deeds first to ascertain ownership. It could be that the space is owned on a shared basis with neighbours. It may be possible to buy them out on one of two bases – either for a cash sum (agreed and dealt with by your lawyer) or by assuming all future responsibility for maintenance and entering into a legally binding repair, upkeep and ownership contract. Caution is our *mot du jour* – be aware of everything before you let your imagination run wild.

Seeing the potential

The one thing you need if you are going to be successful in the property game is imagination. The other thing is chutzpah. Can you spot the potential where others see only the drawbacks? And are you prepared to go all out for it?

Let's say that you come across a run-down, detached, six-bedroom mansion with a large garden that nobody seems to want. It was divided into bed-sits 20 years ago and has been occupied ever since by generations of students. What would you do with it to make it into a comfortable family home? Create an open-plan living area and add a completely new kitchen? Put in a couple of en suite bathrooms? Turn one of the bedrooms into an office or study? Landscape the garden with a separate play area for the children? Or maybe it would be more profitable to turn the mansion into two luxury flats with off-street parking. Could you sell off some of the land to a developer? Or maybe you could develop the plot yourself. What about applying for planning permission to pull the old house down and put six brand-new ones in its place? This is when you do your area-profiling to see what people moving into the locality will be looking for. For example, it makes more sense to keep a large house, perfect for a young family, just as it is if family houses are in short supply in the immediate area.

Don't get carried away with your plans, though, for this is also where you do your sums to work out what is going to give you the best return on your investment. Few of us have a bottomless pit of cash, so your money must be spent wisely. In short, don't think about installing that dream £20,000 kitchen in a house that's worth just £40,000, because you simply won't get your investment back! Often the simplest, and definitely the cheapest, way of changing a room's identity is with a pot of paint and a paintbrush, which is

▶ Often developing space is about more than simply changing decor. Here, for example, adding a window to a galley kitchen has changed the whole dimension of the room.

good news if your budget for development isn't big. So if the property you're looking at is old and ugly, try to see beneath the surface and imagine what it will look like when a lick of paint brings out fresh character and boosts its real appeal. Remember, success is only failure turned inside out. *Every* opportunity should be examined.

As a general rule virtually every property will find a buyer in the end, no matter what condition it is in. After all, we have all read about people buying a 'broom cupboard' in Knightsbridge or a derelict croft on a remote Scottish island. It's all about people's dreams and aspirations and the way these relate to the laws of supply and demand. But having said that, we know that some properties get stuck on the market for an awfully long time. Why should this be? Well, if a property isn't selling it's invariably because it appears to be overpriced compared to the competition. There are two solutions to this: either the price should come down to a more realistic level or the property should be improved to add value. In these circumstances, if you're a buyer you should try to get the price down and if you're a seller you should give your property a make-over (see page 134).

Offers, bids and valuations

One of the most stressful aspects of buying a property is deciding how much you should offer to secure it. We all know people who have got this wrong and have lost their dream home as a result. Common sense dictates that any purchase is only worth what you are willing to pay for it, so decide on your top price and stick to it. Don't let anyone persuade you to push up your offer if you know you can't afford to, and, if you haven't made up your mind yet, don't listen to them when they tell you the house is perfect for you. There are several little tricks that can be played to ensure you get a little nearer your goal – and we shall come to these later – but in the first instance it's all about knowing when something is right for you.

Do your homework, again

Before you decide how much to offer for a property go back and do your area-profiling again. Ask all the local estate agents what sort of prices they are currently getting, and how long it is taking on average to achieve a sale. In other words, are the properties being snapped up overnight or are they hanging around? If it's the former you could find yourself in competition with other buyers and that will push the prices up, and if it's the latter you know you have room to manoeuvre. Although you may already know the answers to some of your questions, it will do no harm to go over them again to make sure you have all the latest information so that you can make an informed decision.

The offer itself

In Scotland vendors tend to sell their properties by asking for offers over a given 'start' price, and it is not uncommon for buyers to bid 10%, 20% and in some cases even 30% in excess of this. The disadvantage of this system is that no one, not even your lawyer or selling agent, can suggest amendments to your offer to give you a better chance of success. Offering 'blind' you could actually be paying a substantial amount over the odds to secure the deal. However, at least every buyer is in the same position ... In many respects, Scotland's 'offers over' scenario is similar to the English 'sealed bids' (see opposite), which are becoming increasingly common as the competitive market surges forward.

In the rest of Britain the asking price is usually a fair indication of what the vendor expects. In effect, unless an agent has seriously misread the

▲ When trying to ascertain what your offer should be, take into account purchase prices for similar properties in the area, how stiff the competition is likely to be and how much you really want the place.

market, a £100,000 house will generally attract offers of just that, give or take a few thousand. However, in times of high demand and scarce supply agents sometimes go for a system of 'sealed bids' or 'best and final offers'. This dreaded scenario has become the scourge of buyers as everyone is literally bidding blind. The agent sets a deadline and all the potential buyers submit their offers on a particular property, in writing, by that date. The 'best' offer then secures the deal. The 'best' offer may not necessarily be the highest offer, though. Other factors, such as the buyer's willingness to agree to the vendor's dates for the exchange of contracts, for example, might be deemed more important than an extra couple of thousand on the price.

Tips for making a successful bid

1 Be a cash buyer. This shows the vendor that you're serious about your buying intent. And as there won't be a delay while you secure your finances, they should be less worried that you may pull out. It will also speed up the legal process and contracts will be exchanged more quickly.

2 Be a first-time buyer. This is attractive to a vendor as you won't have to wait to sell your own home before the purchase process can begin. Being in a chain can be a nightmare for both vendors and buyers.

3 Give your offer an unusual edge. If you have decided on, say, £91,000, add an extra £100 or so – it might just help to pull you ahead in the race. An offer of £91,155 won't break the bank but it might just make all the difference, especially if you are involved in a sealed-bids situation.

4 Be flexible about dates and timing. If you can accommodate the vendor's wishes and agree to tie in with their time schedule you will have an advantage over other buyers who may be trying to inflict *their* preferred schedule on the vendor. Some vendors may want to complete virtually overnight and some may be aiming for a specific date but with a longer lead time, while others may not be able to afford to commit themselves at the beginning because they are buying as well as selling. So make sure you know what your vendor's circumstances are, and try to fit in with what they want as much as possible.

5 Try not to base your offer on too many conditions. If you say that you will buy the property as long as the vendor carries out certain repairs, for example, or only if they include the carpets and curtains, are your conditions reasonable? You will have to do a little amateur psychology. Some people won't mind a bit of haggling but others could be irritated and look for a different buyer. Another option is to make your offer 'subject to survey'. This means that after your report is complete, you harvest all the information and offer accordingly, making any financial amendments you see fit. However, vendors are likely to be wary of such offers and may, in the meantime, accept a more concrete, less conditional bid.

6 Look into the future. This is our biggest tip when it comes to placing successful bids. People are always asking us how much we think they should offer for a particular property, especially when there is a lot of competition and they have been asked to make a sealed bid. Our advice is simple: offer what you feel the house is worth to you. But, and it's a very big 'but', imagine how you'll feel if, at close of offers, you discover you've missed out on the home of your dreams. Would you regret *not* having added an extra few hundred to your offer, or even a thousand or so?

Successful and failed bids

After making an initial verbal offer for the property to the vendor, there's a regimented proceedure that should always be followed. Your finance should theoretically already be in place (if you're a cash buyer you should have the money available and if you're borrowing you should have a current mortgage

offer) before you make your offer. Assuming it is, the next step is to make a
formal bid. This means informing the selling agent of your interest and giving
them your solicitor's details. And then you wait to see if your offer is accepted …

   Of course, your offer may not be accepted. If it isn't, ask your estate
agent why (it could just be bad luck) and then think about what to do next.
If the property is still on the market you could increase your offer, but do
calculate your financial situation carefully before upping your price.

Surveys and valuation reports

If your offer has been accepted the next step is to get the property surveyed
and valued. Go on, admit it – the very mention of the 's' word sends shivers
down your spine. Well, calm down. If you're buying a property it's the
surveyor's job to protect you, and his report is vital – although your dream
home looks perfect to you it may be hiding serious structural faults, which
would cost a fortune to put right after you've moved in.

   Don't confuse valuation reports with structural surveys. If you're taking
out a mortgage your lender will get their own surveyor to do a valuation
report on the property. This is not a thorough survey – just a basic check to
make sure the place has no major faults, that you're not paying more than it's
worth and that the lender will get their money back if you can't pay your
mortgage and the property has to be sold again. You'll be charged from £150
to £200 for a valuation report, depending on the size of the property and
where you live, and you should automatically get sent a copy.

   But while the valuation report keeps the lender happy, a structural survey
gives you peace of mind. You find a surveyor to do it, you pay for it, and it's
up to you to make sure you understand it and take note of its findings.

Different types of survey

There are two main types of survey – a home buyer's report and a full
structural survey, sometimes called a building survey. Which one you choose
depends on the age and type of property you're buying. Some people say that
a home buyer's report is adequate if you're buying a new (post-1930s)
property, whereas if you're buying an older place, or somewhere that has been
converted, you ought to get a full structural survey.

   Our advice would be: don't skimp. We all want to keep costs down, but
the money you spend on a survey could save a lot of heartache later on. Buying
a place of your own is the biggest investment you'll ever make, so grit your
teeth and pay up for a proper investigation to make sure it's also your best one.

Home buyer's report

This is the most basic kind of survey. The surveyor will be looking for obvious problems, but won't be examining a house in detail – when he goes round a property he's basically ticking boxes on a standard form. For instance, he'll check for signs of damp and for obvious cracks or problems with the structure, but he won't lift carpets to examine the floorboards, move furniture or climb a ladder to take a closer look at the roof.

The home buyer's report will give you an idea of how much the property's worth and whether it's generally in a good state of repair, but it's not a comprehensive survey and is not intended to be. You're likely to come across phrases like 'To the best of my knowledge …' and 'At the time of my report there were no immediate signs of …' Disclaimers like this are partly put in to protect a surveyor in case you decide to sue him in a year's time. But it's also because these guys don't have X-ray vision; if a wall looks OK you can't expect a surveyor doing this sort of basic report to be able to judge whether there's a problem with the cavity insulation.

The big attraction of a home buyer's report is that it's the cheap option. Expect to pay at least 3% of the asking price, so if the property is on sale for £100,000 your report will cost anything from £300 to £450.

Full structural survey

As the name implies this is the most thorough – and expensive – option. You can get a full structural survey carried out on any type of property, but it's essential if you're buying an old building or one that's listed, or one that has been converted or altered in any way.

Full structural surveys rarely cost less than £600 nowadays, and you could pay as much as £1000 in an expensive area. But what you're paying for is detail, and a pretty accurate idea of how much it would cost to put any problems right. Whereas a home buyer's report might say that some windows show signs of decay, a full structural report would mention which windows are particularly bad, why the problem has come about and what repairs are necessary. It should also give you an idea of how much the work would cost. The surveyor will test walls for damage and timbers for signs of woodworm or dry rot, get into the roof space and look under accessible floorboards. He'll also comment on any damp-proofing or insulation, and recommend further inspection by specialists if necessary. The only things a full structural survey won't cover are the electrics, plumbing and gas; the surveyor can give an opinion on the general condition of these services – for instance, pointing out that wiring looks old or sockets are cracked – but isn't qualified to do more than that.

Another bonus of a full structural survey is that you get information about the surrounding area. You're partly paying for the surveyor's specialist local knowledge and experience, so if he knows of any problems with subsidence, flooding or anything else he'll pass it on. You might think the small stream in the garden is a pretty feature when you buy your home in spring, but fast-forward six months and you'll be grateful your surveyor warned you it could turn into a raging torrent in November.

▲ Your potential new property might look well-tended on the outside, but it's worth getting a full structural survey to check out the fabric and foundations.

Deciphering a survey

- Don't be phased by jargon. Full structural surveys can get very technical, even going into the specific types of brick and mortar used in the construction of the house, so don't get bogged down by detail.
- If there seem to be endless problems with the property, don't panic. Remember the surveyor doesn't want to be landed with a legal bill in a year's time, so, to cover his back, he'll point out even the smallest problem. Read the report through several times, and pick out the important things (these should be summarized in a conclusion).
- Be realistic about what matters. If the surveyor says a window frame is starting to rot or that the chimney flashing needs attention, this doesn't mean the place will crash around your ears in the next few months. On the other hand, if he finds damp or thinks there might be woodworm in the attic, this kind of thing could cost you a lot of money, so you need to do something about it straight away.

Five things you need to know about surveying

1 Talk to the surveyor before they go to the property, so you know what they're going to do. If you've seen anything you're not sure about – loose mortar, cracked walls – ask them to check it out. Mention any plans you've got for the future, such as a loft conversion or an extension to one side of the property, and get their opinion on whether they are viable.

2 Appreciate that 'valuation' and 'sale price' aren't always the same thing. Because of the quirks of the property market, at any given time it's possible for a property to sell for more or less than its official valuation – an owner might decide to add another £20,000 to the estimated sale price given by an estate agent, just to see if anyone bites, and, in a buoyant market, may get lucky. However, a surveyor will be using his specialist local knowledge to say how much your property is worth, so you can be sure you're not being fleeced.

3 Don't be alarmed when you get the report back. Full structural surveys are long documents, but that's because they're packed with information and it's all designed to help you. If you've got queries or don't understand what's been written, call the surveyor and talk it through. Don't be embarrassed about doing this; you're not in the business, so why should you be expected to understand the difference between a purlin and a soffit? Also, factor in the possibility of having to instruct and pay for additional specialist reports, if required, such as timber, roofing and electrical investigation.

4 Some people use a bad survey to renegotiate on price, but there's no point doing this unless the surveyor has picked up some serious structural defects. If he reckons you'll have to spend £5000 on damp-proofing or repairs to the roof, ask to have that amount taken off the asking price. If it's just a few hundred quid here and there on smaller problems, you're unlikely to get anywhere.

5 A survey is a bit like an MOT on your car – it shows the condition of a property on a particular day, but there's no guarantee that problems won't crop up 12 months later. Things wear out and bad weather damages properties, so if your move is dragging on over months you ought to consider having the survey updated.

Finding a surveyor

You need someone who belongs to the Royal Institute of Chartered Surveyors – they'll have either MRICS or FRICS after their name. This means the surveyor should abide by a code of conduct, and if they miss something there's a formal complaints proceedure you can follow. Estate agents have lists of recommended surveyors or you could get some names from the RICS on 0870 3331600.

Gazumping and gazundering

Gazumping occurs when the vendor suddenly decides, before contracts have been exchanged, to accept a higher offer than the one they accepted from you. It is a term with which most of us are now familiar, but gazundering is a more recent phenomenon that fewer of us will recognize but which can have equally awful circumstances, this time for the vendor. Gazundering occurs when the buyer, at the last moment, informs the vendor that they still wish to conclude the sale, but at a lower price than that which was orginally agreed.

What happens next

Once you've negotiated on the survey and any outstanding queries have been sorted out, the next step is to exchange contracts. Your solicitor deals with this, but it's important you understand what's going on: the contract is the official document that transfers ownership of the property and you'll be sent a copy to sign. Your solicitor and the vendor's solicitor usually exchange over the phone, verbally agreeing that the deal has been done and, on the same day, you hand over 10% of the purchase price, held by the vendor's solicitor as a down payment on the sale. Finally, a completion date is agreed – usually in four weeks, but sometimes sooner. If you aren't selling and your vendor isn't buying another property, getting to this stage should be relatively stress-free but, if you're buying in a chain, things are less predictable. When a number of people are buying and selling different properties, below or above you, several transactions are dependent on each other. All the different deals must be done simultaneously and all contracts exchanged on the same day. Most chains work out in the end, but it's frustrating being stuck in the middle of one.

Once you've exchanged, you need to hire a crack removals team or enlist some loyal friends to shift your possessions into your new home when you complete. Finally, crack open a bottle of vino. Well done, it's time to celebrate!

Hartledon Road, HARBORNE, BIRMINGHAM

Property profile

A two-reception, two-bedroom, two-storey terraced house with tired and dirty decoration, ineffectual heating, cheap dated kitchen and bathroom, with overgrown gardens at the front and the rear. Offers around £100,000. Freehold.

As soon as the house was marketed there was considerable interest and offers went to sealed private bids. Well before this 'closing date' we made an offer of £98,000 on a '24-hour acceptance' basis to try and convince the vendors to take the house off the market. We hoped they might think that a bird in the hand was worth two in the bush. This is often a workable idea, but on this occasion the owner refused and decided to hold tight ... We then offered £103,000 and were successful. Here are our sums:

Buying price:	£103,000
Buying costs:	£2000
Development costs:	£20,000
Selling costs:	£3000
Selling price:	£143,000
Profit:	£15,000

We decided to put our first foot on the 'ladder of speculation' with a property priced at £100,000, and began our search. We were determined not to bite off more than we could chew, so we wanted to find a project that would result in a sizeable return without killing us into the bargain. Careful consideration suggested we should buy in an up-and-coming area (a 'hot spot') and that we should aim the fruits of our labours at the 'first-time buyer' or 'young professional' market.

Location

Having heard about Birmingham's renaissance, we decided to pay a visit to get a feel for what was happening. To put it mildly, our eyes were opened. Once considered to have one of the most pitiful and dismal centres in Britain, the Birmingham of the twenty-first century has become a vibrant and exciting destination.

Selfridges and Harvey Nichols have joined Emporio Armani and Terence Conran as the city transforms into a happening hotbed for culture, commerce and leisure. Excited, we decided to join this new investing confidence by securing a few 'city shares' ourselves.

We spoke to developers, retail giants, town planners and locals to discover that new investment would bring an estimated 12,000 jobs, which would have a positive effect on the demand for property both in and around the city centre. House prices have already improved and, with Birmingham's £1 billion redevelopment due to continue, it is predicted that they will continue to rise and that demand for suitable properties will exceed supply.

Why Harborne?

Birmingham certainly appeared to be a great place for us to kick off, but it's a big old city so it was rather difficult to determine where best to start. Further investigation highlighted several areas 'on the up', but one zone in particular caught our attention. Three miles from the city centre and close to Birmingham University and the Queen Elizabeth Hospital lies Harborne, an area of quality shops, restaurants and quaint local pubs. The building style is predominantly Victorian terraced, but there are also some detached and semi-detached houses and apartments both old and new.

Harborne is a not only a desirable area for 'bright young things' with a disposable income, but it also offers long-term benefits in the shape of good schools and comprehensive public amenities. Recently, Marks & Spencer opened a food hall there, which indicates that the area is consolidating and that there's money about. Other indications are evidence that Harborne homes sell quickly (we confirmed this by talking to several estate agents), the fact that everyone seemed to be working on exterior and interior improvements, and the liberal dappling of smart cars and well-dressed people out and about in the streets.

After searching for properties adjacent to Harborne high street we found them too expensive for our purposes, with prices hovering in excess of £125,000. Undeterred, we plodded onwards and eventually found a perfect property on Hartledon Road, a Victorian terraced house which, while not on the immediate drag, was still within easy walking distance of Harborne's main thoroughfares. Bingo!

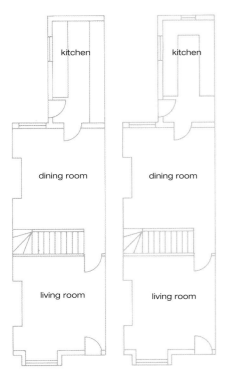

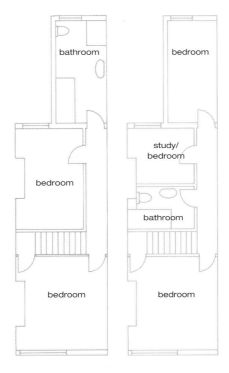

◀ We kept the ground floor layout as it was, apart from converting the understairs cupboard into a useful cloakroom (see page 84 left). Upstairs, the second bedroom was divided to accommodate an internal bathroom and a study/bedroom. The original bathroom became the second bedroom.

GROUND FLOOR before (left) and after

FIRST FLOOR before (left) and after

Our plans

We planned to change this two-bedroom terraced property from a tired, neglected house into a clean, crisp and contemporary pied-à-terre aimed at a young professional who, while not necessarily design aware, would appreciate high standards. Not only did we want to design a fresher home, we also wanted to carve up the available space to create the potential for three comfortable bedrooms and a new bathroom.

Apart from some minor rising-damp problems that were discovered during the full structural survey, the actual foundations of the house were sound. All we needed to do was remove imperfections and update the look.

The kitchen

In the kitchen we made huge changes, redefining the space from a tired galley, complete with old 'farmhouse'-style units, to a clean and precise room to die for. When budget is limited, it's a good idea to accessorize lower cost items with luxurious additions, so we dressed our value MFI kitchen with stainless-steel circular sinks and real timber worktops to pump up the 'wow' factor. With the emphasis on budget, the existing floor tiles were cleaned and regrouted to stunning effect.

In any room it is important to maximize not only space but light. After much deliberation we decided to punch a hole into the back south-facing wall and put in an additional window, thereby adding greatly to the available light and at the same time providing a mind trick that made the kitchen register as being larger than it actually was (see page 41). Previously, anyone entering the room was met with a flat dark wall, but after work was

completed eye lines projected all the way to the bottom of the garden. If you intend tackling such a job seek approval first from your local planning office and, if necessary, employ the services of a qualified builder.

Sushi-bar chic came in the form of open shelving, perfect for displaying crockery and glasses and, by adding a Smeg fridge, we weren't just equipping a kitchen, we were leaving vital style clues, all of which spelt out quality of life – something everybody wants from their home, no?

The living room

In the living room wallpaper was stripped and replaced with newly plastered walls painted taupe, the perfect neutral base for a variety of styles. The insubstantial fireplace with its gas fire was removed and a previously bricked-up arched fireplace exposed (see page 96). It is important to make the most of your home's original features. But how can you be sure what's lurking behind boarded-up walls? We discovered our arch after visiting our new next-door neighbours to spy out the features in their identical terraced house. Not only were we introducing ourselves – we were also on a vital fact-finding mission.

Back in our house, an expensive-looking cream carpet was installed. Chrome electrical fittings throughout provided a visible quality-of-work guarantee for the rest of the property, acting like eye-catching buttons on a suit.

The dining room

In the dining room the chimney was swept to allow for good air circulation, and the budget reproduction fireplace was replaced with a traditional cast-iron surround housing a living-flame gas fire installed by a registered gas fitter.

◀ Predominantly an exercise in redecoration, this cold uninviting room was transformed into a comfortable and stylish dining room.

Putting in this kind of fireplace is a great idea and needn't cost the earth – we purchased ours from an online salvage yard. Simple coving was added where the walls joined the ceiling to provide a vital additional feature and the taupe wall colour was continued from the living room to provide continuity, only this time it was tempered with red to add eye-catching drama (see above).

Bedroom one

Upstairs, the master bedroom was painted warm yellow to enliven and energize (see page 54). Adding an inexpensive picture-rail provided period detail and offered an opportunity to provide decorating 'interest' with paint – we coloured the ceiling matt white, which effectively expanded the dimensions. Using an unpatterned carpet completed the look and provided perfect softness on which to pad around.

Converting bedroom two

To adapt the existing accommodation to tie in with today's market needs, we decided to convert the existing bathroom into a bedroom and subdivide the second bedroom into a bathroom and study/bedroom three. Confusing, huh? Well, let us explain, as the reasons were actually simple:

- The bathroom had previously been a bedroom when the property had an outdoor toilet, so we knew there was enough space.
- Demographic research (we drew our conclusions from information harvested from estate agents) suggested that our buyer would require two bedrooms and a study/third bedroom.
- Our plans were cheaper than a loft conversion and the loft-potential was left intact for the next buyer.

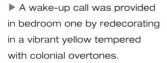

▶ A wake-up call was provided in bedroom one by redecorating in a vibrant yellow tempered with colonial overtones.

The work to make these changes had to be approved by planning and building control but was relatively straightforward. The bathroom sanitarywares, shower and redundant pipework were removed, the plumbing was redirected to the new bathroom and the frosted window was replaced with a double-glazed standard unit. The lino flooring was replaced with carpet and we opted for a sand-coloured scheme.

The bathroom

The new bathroom was created by cropping one-third of the floor space from what had been the second bedroom in the original configuration. A stud-partition wall was built and the plumbing was redirected. To keep costs down we even decided to reuse the bath, sink and toilet, and after a thorough clean they were as good as new! Because the original door to bedroom two (now our study/bedroom three) remained exactly where it was, we had to form a door to access the new bathroom from the landing. As the corridor wall wasn't load-bearing this was a

relatively simple procedure, but the necessary planning consents still had to be obtained.

We chose white and aqua mosaic tiles. Practical as well as beautiful, mosaic tiles are perceived as being more expensive than they actually are and, with mirrors cleverly embedded in them, gave the bathroom a modern edge (see page 84 right). We changed the fittings, installed ventilation and added a smart new toilet seat.

To limit costs, we chose budget modern ceiling lamps to flood the room with illumination and allow for such pursuits as shaving and making-up. We added a tiled surface for must-have toiletries, and a frosted glass counter over the sink. The addition of door hooks, towel-rails and a toilet-roll holder provided sparkling eye candy and finished off the look perfectly.

The study/bedroom three

The study, carved from the original bedroom two, was coloured to feel like a haven – the perfect place in which to work from home (see page 101). Chanel 'Pour Monsieur' grey was the key colour used to instil an unfussy and efficient personality. Painting one zone with a dominant shade and the others with a lighter grey-white opened up the narrow space and directed the viewer's attention to one wall.

Outside

We removed trees and creepers to expose brickwork and to make the property appear larger. We replaced ugly crazy-paving with clean concrete steps and the windows and door were repainted (see page 1). Simplicity was key – we didn't want our property on Hartledon Road to stick out; it had to complement the other houses in the terrace and not compete with them visually.

The rear garden was cleared and redundant outhouses were replaced with a patio. A simple lawn proved to be a great way of hiding bumps and lumps – think of a rug over a broken floorboard and you should get the idea. Having a patio was a great bonus as it gave us somewhere extra to dress – a table and chairs made it into a valuable additional dining area for the summer months.

Estate agency time

We first invited a couple of agents to value the property as a blank canvas – but one that was fully restored – before we dressed it. They concurred that it would be worth between £127,500 and £130,000 – a higher than average market value due to the 'quality inclusions' and the 'attention to detail'. Hmm. Although we were satisfied (ish) with these initial valuations, we believed that the property would sell for more if we 'merchandised' it .

At this point we pinpointed one agent to represent us, chosen because of his approach and personality, because he stocked similar properties to ours and because we were impressed by his sales literature. Before inviting him back, we dressed the house to impress with simple furnishings and accessories. What we couldn't borrow from friends we bought cheaply, adding furnishings that complemented the existing colour scheme – modern plain sofas with leather club chairs in the living room and a glass table in the study with minimalist CD and media storage. In the second bedroom we positioned a divan in the middle of the wall (see page 106). This gave it a 'daybed' feel and it became central to the room rather than being pushed into one corner. In a small space like this it was vital that nothing dominated, so we kept things pared down and simple. We also included quality-of-life 'signifiers' throughout the house, like fresh-coffee makers, olive oils and balsamic vinegar in the kitchen, the 'designer' laptop in the study and piles of soft linen in the bedrooms. Remember: presentation is important in any sales situation, especially if you want to maximize profits.

Second time around and the valuation was an altogether different story, with the agent projecting the property up to the £139,000 mark. Result! We opted for an advert in the local paper, followed by viewings over the following weeks. Within a fortnight we had several offers including one for a whopping great £143,000 – a serious bid if ever there was one. Not only was it the highest bid, it was also the highest quality bid – from a chain-free, first-time, young professional buyer with finances already in place. What's more, he could move in within a month.

Four weeks on and the deed was done – we concluded the sale, handed over the keys and received the money. We were up and running again.

LIV

Whether you've just bought a new property and are deciding what to do with it, or want to make changes to your existing home with a view to selling for optimum profit one day, this section will give you all the inspiration and practical advice you need. Follow our guide to key improvements for your property and you'll create the perfect living space. We'll also let you into many of our trade secrets and with time, and just a little effort on your part, the value of your home will soar.

I N G

Where to start

Most of us see having a comfortable house as a vital part of our lives. But for many of us, having a home that is not only comfortable but is also *beautiful* is becoming even more important. As TV programmes like ours – as well as the many interior design magazines for which we write – show we are all beginning to expect just a little bit extra when it comes to nest-building. We travel more widely, we read more about the way other people live, and so we demand more. We know a lot about the rich and famous and these days we want a little bit of that special lifestyle magic for ourselves. And if *we* work hard we expect our homes to work hard for us.

Most people would admit that their home could be improved in some way. Does your kitchen really provide all the modern amenities you want? Is your garden big enough? Do you have all the bedrooms you need? Do you have space for your work? If the answer to any of these questions is no you need to work out what you can do to improve your space, and consequently your life. On the other hand, if you've bought a property with a view to improving it then selling on, you should make sure it has everything a potential owner might need, whether they're a family or a professional couple. You'll have to learn to be dispassionate and to consider what buyers are likely to want, not simply what makes living there better for you.

▼ Don't make changes for the sake of it. Your new property might need little more than a lick of paint to bring it up to date.

How do you decide whether to make any changes?

Unfortunately, there's no set answer to this – it's a question that will elicit a different response on almost every occasion. If, for example, you've just bought a bargain three-bedroom semi in Wolverhampton for £55,000 there are certain things you could do to increase its value straight away: a new kitchen or bathroom would almost certainly be a good investment. But if you spend, say, £30,000 on an open-air swimming pool in the back garden you would be unlikely to recover your costs. The potential buying market simply won't have the available funds to cover your asking price, which will have to be increased to cover your costs. In general, flamboyant enhancements only work in areas where prospective buyers have unlimited budgets. So, by all means add that fabulous pool, but only if you're developing a Surrey mansion with a £1,000,000 price tag!

Tailoring your approach

To clarify exactly what your options are, we have described four scenarios and highlighted which sections of this chapter will help you most, depending on which group you fall into.

1 You already own a property and are happy living there. However, you want to make some improvements, particularly to the lifestyle areas, such as the kitchen, living room (if you want to create some workspace, see page 100) and garden. This is your home, so you want to make it as comfortable and personal as possible to improve your quality of life.

2 You want to sell your current home. You need to step away from your own residential requirements and consider what a potential new owner would expect. You will need to improve outdated aspects and make sure every element of your home is up to scratch (see Cosmetic changes on page 62 and Staging on page 138).

3 You've bought a new property to live in. You may well need to make big structural changes to suit your needs (see Structural changes on page 70).

4 You've bought a new property to develop and sell on. You will have to think about your market and consider what structural changes you may need to plan for to ensure your property fits the bill. What does the locality demand? An extra bedroom? A conservatory (see page 111)? Time to get planning!

Assessing your own property

Staying put – group 1

If you fit into the first group, it's time to assess what changes you could make, to up the pleasure factor at home or simply to make your property run more smoothly. Maintenance and modernization are critical both to ensure that your home remains a comfortable place to live in and that your biggest investment is safeguarded for the future. You will appreciate the benefits in the long run and the value of your home should increase to boot.

Honest work

However you choose to develop a property, whether to improve your own lifestyle or for financial gain, you should always do it with integrity, honesty and care. It will give you so much more satisfaction to know that you have put your best effort into the work. And, on a more pragmatic note, you don't want to risk giving a buyer in the future any reason to blame you if things go wrong. As we were picking our way through the property-development maze for *The Million Pound Property Experiment*, we were always careful not to compromise our standards. While it was important to achieve the optimum selling price, it was similarly crucial that the build standard of each property was impeccable.

Selling on – group 2

If you feel the time has come to sell your home take a look at each room – what do you see? Now be honest! What you *should* see is a vision of tight design perfection but what you probably *will* see (especially if you are reading this book) is a space that needs identity. Perhaps it's a sum of its unfinished parts, a testament to depleted enthusiasm that sells you – and your home – short. Perhaps it's simply a series of rooms decorated some time ago that says more about your past than the present. Try to be impartial. Be brutally honest. Step outside your own life and take a look in. Do you like what you see? If not, you have quite a bit of work ahead of you. The difference between what your home is worth today and what it could fetch after a few weekends of concentrated effort could be several thousand pounds. If you have never sold a property before, be warned! Potential buyers can be very hard. They will expect a perfect home.

So what should you do to prepare your home for visual interrogation by an army of expectant buyers? Well, in short, as much as possible: everything you can afford to do should be done. We're not suggesting gold-plating your taps or putting in a tennis court, but you should at least tackle all those little jobs you have been putting off for years. You might have been perfectly happy to live with blocked gutters or peeling wallpaper but a buyer will identify these as problems straight away and could make them an excuse to haggle on the price. Unfinished equals unloved in our opinion, so get cracking.

Moving and improving – group 3

If you've just bought a new property and intend to live there for some time don't be afraid to spend money on improvements – remember the property is not just an investment, but your home as well. You can offset any repair costs against accommodation costs saved.

Depending upon the level of development required to turn your property into your dream home, there are several different approaches required. Bear in mind that the level of work will differ from property to property. Some houses will need only a quick lick of paint to make them habitable, while others will require substantial alterations. It may be that you can carry out the entire redesign programme with an army of willing friends and gallons of paint. You may have to learn a host of new DIY techniques, gleaned from manuals and shows such as ours. But be realistic – the work may be beyond your personal talents and you might have to call in a team of qualified engineers, plumbers, joiners and electricians before you can get your project off the ground. Remember, it's better to be safe than sorry.

Making a profit – group 4

Let us assume for the moment that you have just bought your first property with the sole purpose of doing it up and selling it on as soon as possible. Will you be able to get away with a quick change of décor or will you have to make some more radical changes? The key to this decision is to examine the competition and get a feel for the look that works best in your area. As a broad generalization, using London as a barometer, we can identify several popular trends. In Chelsea or South Kensington, for example, a generic theme that works well is a timeless ivory and gold mix dressed with elegantly swagged curtains and simple dark-wood finishes. Like it or not, it's a look that can be seen filling the windows of almost every estate agent from SW3 to SW7. Move eastwards to Docklands or Shoreditch and the feel is distinctly cooler: think timber floors, limestone finishes, glass sinks and stainless steel. In the suburbs it's all terracotta tiles and coir matting on the floors, rattan or leather furniture and Smeg fridges. So find out what the neighbours are doing and then do it yourself – only better.

Are the rules set in stone?

You could argue that when it comes to doing up a property there are no fixed rules and it's all a matter of personal taste. If you like leopardskin prints and copper mixed with black ash and marble who's to say you won't find a buyer who likes that style too? But common sense should tell you that if the way you present your home is too idiosyncratic you will automatically put a lot of people off. It's a good idea to remember this, even if you're not planning on selling your property yet – one day you probably will, so bear this in mind when making any major changes.

Budget

Don't forget you need to work out a specific budget for each project. There are, of course, no fixed rules that determine what it will cost to redesign your property. In our own experience our budgets, created during the initial planning stages of redesign, have often been exceeded by between 5% and, wait for it, 40% – ouch! So, as we say in Scotland, 'go canny': be prepared and spend carefully.

Cosmetic changes

For you to live comfortably in your own home we reckon there has to be a prevalent element of 'you'. There's little point being a slave to decorative trends if the result is an environment that could make the front page of *Elle Decoration* but leaves you cold. If you don't intend to move on just yet, keep the look simple but thoroughly comfortable. A palette of soft creams and natural shades is best, as it can be adjusted seasonally as the mood takes you. When you come to sell, if you've played the understated card from the beginning it won't take much to give your home an up-to-date look.

In our other life as designers/presenters of BBC1's *Trading Up* we demonstrate how, with a budget of £500 and in 24 hours, you can prepare your home for sale, thus making a huge difference to its marketability. A typical episode involves highlighting – and remedying – weak spots, minimizing serious problems, redecorating, decluttering and styling. Our best result so far was when we did up a mansion apartment that had been stuck on the market for an incredible 18 months. The place actually had great potential but this was hidden under dingy paintwork, overwhelming clutter, which spilled from every room into a narrow hallway, a dated kitchen decorated with dark grey ceramic tiles and a bedroom that had more

▼ A neutral room will provide optimum flexibility and the perfect canvas for a variety of looks.

furniture than Brick Lane market. The remedial work we did was simple: we painted the kitchen tiles with specialist ceramic-tile paint, we redecorated three rooms and recarpeted one and we stripped the apartment of anything that wasn't either beautiful or functional. The owner grew more and more uncomfortable as we proceeded to banish all traces of his personality from his home but he reluctantly gave us his blessing. After all, he *was* desperate to sell … While we were at it we cleaned for Britain, added fresh flowers everywhere and changed the layout of the furniture so that potential buyers could walk to the windows and enjoy the beautiful countryside views. With our £500 well spent, we closed the door on a successful make-over that resulted in a sale the very next day – at the asking price.

Carnarvon Road, STRATFORD, LONDON

Property profile

A one-reception, three-bedroom flat on the top two floors of a Victorian town house with a small front garden. Offers around £137,500. Leasehold.

The property was a mangy old mongrel that had been tenanted for years and now looked filthy and utterly knackered. But we fell in love with its amazing potential instantly. We couldn't resist the collapsed ceiling in an upstairs room, the bodged kitchen or the bathroom that was lying in pieces. Spread out over two floors, we knew it could *all* eventually be made gorgeous.

We decided it was definitely a good option at the market price of £137,500, as we anticipated an ultimate sell-out price of somewhere approaching £200,000. Here are our sums:

Buying price:	£137,500
Buying costs:	£2500
Development costs:	£59,700
Selling costs:	£5300
Selling price:	£215,000
Profit:	£10,000

Finally, after weeks of searching, we found property number two tucked discreetly in the shadows of a sky-scraping tower block in London's East End. The top two floors of a honey-coloured Victorian town house, its condition could only be described as desperate. No, make that desperate to the power of 10. Part of the rental sector for many years it was trainspotting, of the Irvine Welsh variety, personified. On the plus side, at the time we were searching, everyone in the property know was mumbling that Stratford could be the next area of London to 'go' (that's 'pop into life' in layman's terms) so we felt rather excited.

Location

Stratford in east London was, and still is, seriously 'on the up'. Only half an hour's drive from the throbbing city centre, its appeal has been rising for some time due partly to what we call the 'ripple effect' – the knock-on 'up pricing' that spreads from one popular area to the next. We were excited by the popularity of 'buzz' areas in the East End, like Shoreditch and Clerkenwell, and hoped that people who were priced out there might consider Stratford as an alternative. Having undergone a radical transformation in the past few years to reidentify its centre, Stratford now appeals to those who want a bit of space but don't want to shell out a fortune for the privilege. Transport links are already much improved with the redevelopment of the local bus station and the extension of the Jubilee tube line, and if the proposed Eurostar terminal is built investors are likely to see huge returns. But there's more. For those who like a spot of retail therapy, there is something awesome in store – currently land is being cleared to create the largest shopping centre in the whole of Europe.

Why Carnarvon Road?

Scan around Stratford these days and try and find reasonably priced property and you could become very disheartened. During our search we saw one-bedroom flats for £170,000-plus and we saw two-bedroom flats beginning to scrape £200,000. Anything remotely central in Stratford was already out of our league, and as a result we had to consider side streets that are perhaps a 10-minute walk from the redeveloped area. On the plus side, these secondary streets are home to well-proportioned houses, many of which have fallen into disrepair over the past couple of decades. Hoorah, we were stumbling slowly into developers' paradise …

Our plans

While fantastically interesting, the flat had little going for it in the first instance apart from its potential. Of all the properties we redeveloped throughout the series, this was by far the most needy, requiring rewiring and replumbing amongst other things. However, on the plus side its layout was good and, from a redevelopment point of view, we didn't have to do anything to 'relocate' any of the rooms.

To ascertain who was buying what in Stratford, we went about doing some 'vox pops'. Scary stuff! As any TV presenter will tell you, there's little more unnerving than randomly thrusting a microphone into somebody's face as you can never tell quite what will happen. Positioned at the entrance to Canary Wharf tube station, we did our best to harness a feel for

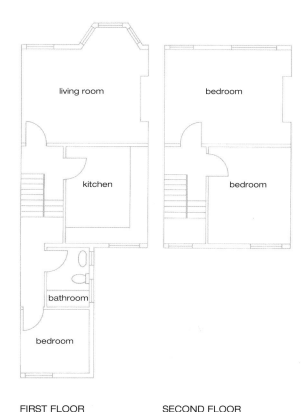

FIRST FLOOR   SECOND FLOOR

▲ The original configuration required no change, leaving us free to concentrate our attention on the three Rs – renovation, repair and redesign.

what people expect from cool inner-city living. We learned that having at least two bedrooms was preferable (so that one could be used as a study or rented to provide income if ever it was required), a modern kitchen with integrated appliances was a must and fittings such as roll-top baths would be manna from design heaven. Colour schemes, we were advised, should be – on the whole – neutral, and space should be open and fluid. Other points raised were high ceilings (a bonus), neutral carpets, quiet location, some outside space – if possible – and good value for money. So we set to work …

The living room

If ever the adage 'If it ain't broke, don't fix it' applied, it was here. OK, so the room looked like the worst student squat you've ever seen, but its heart still had a pulse … vaguely. In layout terms the space had been configured in the best possible way by whoever originally designed the conversion. What's more, it was amply sized and had two large windows – all we had to do was pop in new double glazing, replaster and redecorate (see below and page 126). We opted for smooth seamless laminate flooring and painted the space pure white to optimize all the available light. Clutter was kept to a minimum to allow the room to speak for itself; we added only a sofa, rugs and a low table (and some simple artwork). Carving a hole in the chimney breast created a neat little aperture that could be used for storage or to display fresh flowers or ornaments, etc (see page 63).

The only concession to expense was a Mies van der Rohe Barcelona chair in oxblood that we borrowed. Its inclusion, we hoped, would suggest that the rest of the room – and indeed the flat – had been furnished with expensive 'objets'. Ah, the art of suggestion! The principle that we applied was simple – it's like buying a budget suit from a high street store then adding designer accessories to suggest that the entire outfit is in fact expensive.

The kitchen

There was nothing reusable in the kitchen in any shape or form. Out went the old units, worktop, fridge, cooker and sink. Down came the ceiling, which would have come down anyway without much invitation if anyone had given it so much as a sideways look. Out came the window, which was

so rotted it had been gaffer-taped together by a previous tenant in an apparent attempt to secure it. We rewired, replumbed and installed new lighting. We opted for a mix of cherrywood and aluminium-finish cabinets to create a bright, modern and spacious room. Arranging the units on an L-shape meant we were able to leave enough space for a small table and chairs to be added, to spell out clearly that this was not simply a kitchen but a comfortable kitchen/dining room that offered space to entertain (see page 67).

Because ceramic tiles on the floor might have been too heavy we opted instead for an amazing product by Amtico called 'Iced Glass'. It not only looked stunning but it would 'read' well in the property particulars when the flat

was eventually put up for sale, and would be guaranteed to impress potential buyers.

The bathroom

As with the living room, the basics were perfect – even the plumbing was in the right place. Transforming the bathroom from neglect into cool casual sophistication took little more than common sense. We added 'must have' detail via good-quality sanitarywares and DIY-store tongue-and-groove timber cladding painted soft green. This, with hindsight, was probably the simplest bathroom make-over we tackled throughout the series but, as far as we're concerned, it was the one that created the most dramatic 'before and after'. Aside from the bathroom suite our biggest outlay was on the floor covering but, hey, as we always say, 'If a job's worth doing, it's worth doing gorgeously'! We therefore opted for more of our beloved Amtico, this time specifying a modern take on marble in contrasting shades of pearlescent green and lilac for an attractive mix of neutral New England and fresh inner-city cool (see page 86). We accessorized with a simple white Shaker chair (a £5 junk shop find painted white) and all manner of cute bowls, pretty jars and glass bottles. Again, it's not what you use, it's how you use it – we filled these with supermarket bubble-bath and inexpensive bath salts to create a luxurious indulgent look.

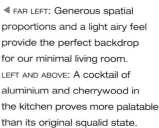

◀ FAR LEFT: Generous spatial proportions and a light airy feel provide the perfect backdrop for our minimal living room. LEFT AND ABOVE: A cocktail of aluminium and cherrywood in the kitchen proves more palatable than its original squalid state.

Bedrooms one and two

To provide a break from the predominantly white scheme in other rooms we added a shot of red to one wall in the smaller bedroom – a signature 'power' colour that would be perceived as a strong statement (see below). In the larger of the two rooms we initially planned soft pink, then later considered soft blue but eventually decided to be gender unspecific and opted for lilac (see page 129 right). Viewers subsequently commented favourably on both rooms, so we think we got it pretty right. It's amazing that simple colour choice can go some of the way to persuading – or dissuading – potential buyers that yours is the home for them.

▼ Don't be afraid to use strong colour in a small room – here a single wall of colour provides enough impact.

Bedroom three ('Utopia')

It was here that we made the most noticeable change. Actually, let us correct ourselves – it was here that Mother Nature had made the most noticeable change. Due to a violent storm a small section of roof had been dislodged and the room had flooded. As a result, the ceiling had collapsed, revealing the 'butterfly' beams above. On our first viewing we thought that this could make for a room with an incredible shape – find a fault, make a feature, we always say. Plasterboarding over the beams without creating a traditional flat ceiling resulted in a wedge-shaped room that, with the addition of two Velux skylights, became a real selling feature of the flat. However – be warned! Any alteration like this may need planning approval so seek out the assistance of your local council. You'll also need the agreement of the leaseholder. The changes involved rather a lot of work, but the 'new' bedroom provided an extra something that we hoped would appeal to potential buyers who fancied the idea of loft-living but didn't quite have the capital to make their dream a reality (see page 69).

Outside

To make a good first impression, we cleaned the exterior of the property to restore the brickwork to its former glory and opted for good-quality budget double-glazing throughout (see page 1). Bearing in mind that our 'vox pops' had said outside space would be a bonus, we ensured that what little terrain we had was made as attractive as possible. The addition of a central flowerbed, a manageable gravelled area and some paving stones turned a once unattractive approach into a positive selling feature, and somewhere to sit when the weather is fine.

UTOPIA

◀ Transforming chaos into calm gave us a unique loft-style space to win purchasers over.

Estate agency time

We felt that the service provided by the estate agent who had sold us the property in the first instance was friendly, helpful and efficient – an approach that mixed knowledge of the local area with just the right amount of salesmanship. Before appointing him to sell on our rebranded apartment we had checked out other estate agents, looking for similarly priced properties. Then we viewed a few of these properties to ascertain how the agents treated potential buyers and how informed they were. This meant that we could make an informed estimate as to how much we expected for our property. Taking into account our agent's advice, we finally decided to market the property at £230,000 – a huge price for the Stratford market, but when you're developing in an up-and-coming area, you have to be brave and push the market limits.

Our agent decided to introduce the property to the market through a series of open-day viewings, during which potential buyers would be invited to attend any time between nine and five. This approach is potentially the most time efficient because it allows the owner to designate one day per week for viewings.

The results of the first viewings weren't great; in fact, many people seemed disappointed that the flat didn't have a proper garden. Aside from that, other comments were mostly favourable, although several viewers remarked on the fact that there was no shower in the bathroom. To rectify this we simply replaced the existing bath taps with a 'telephone'-style shower-and-bath mixer, and put up a snazzy chrome shower-ring complete with curtain.

After six weeks of furious nail-biting and no offers we reduced the asking price to £215,000. Within days we had accepted an offer at asking price from a woman who bought it to house her niece who was going on to further education. The final price wasn't quite as much as we'd hoped for, but it was enough for us to make a reasonable profit.

Structural changes

A £500 make-over may help you achieve a quick sale but probably won't send the value of your property into orbit. Most structural changes, however, while involving major spending, could add value (see Case Study 4 on page 152).

As a general guide, if you buy somewhere with the intention of making money on it, after purchase and renovation costs you should aim for a profit of 15%–20% when you resell. So if you buy a property for £100,000 and spend a further £10,000 doing it up, it would be reasonable to expect to sell for £125,000–£130,000, assuming you've chosen the right property in the right location. This might sound like a modest return on your investment, but it's more than you'd earn in interest from a bank or building society.

If you've bought somewhere with the intention of doing it up and making money, you may have to pay Capital Gains Tax on your profit. The amount payable depends which tax band you fall into and how much profit you make, but you can offset certain expenses, such as buying and selling costs and any money you spent on structural improvements. You're usually exempt from Capital Gains Tax if you live in the property while carrying out the work, and there are other ways of whittling down the bill. The Inland Revenue has leaflets explaining how Capital Gains Tax works, but it's a complicated business, so employ a good accountant and leave it to the experts.

Moving on up

Attic or loft conversions have long been considered a good way of expanding and, as with any move that doesn't involve a change of address, there will be no removal costs and, in turn, no stamp duty to be paid or estate agents to deal with. As with any conversion, you'll need to check on planning consents and safety regulations – you may need to add a fire escape, for example. Some planning authorities will be happier than others to approve the extension – some may be protective of local 'roof lines' (see page 71). As a general guide to how likely it is that your application will be successful, look around the neighbourhood to see how many other homes have undergone transformation. If you share your building with others you probably share ownership of the roof space above. Before going to the expense of calling in planners and architects, ensure that you have legal ownership of the space.

Attic conversions make brilliant playrooms, but do bear in mind that heat rises, so unless ventilation is perfect, your children could get very warm and uncomfortable. Make sure the design allows for free passage of air and includes windows. Extra bedrooms also slot perfectly into roof space. Costs

will vary according to the level of work required but, as a rough guide, adding an extra couple of bedrooms and perhaps a loo will cost you anything from £15,000 – the sky literally is the limit. Basic reconfigurations with flat Velux-type windows (and without dormer windows) will be at the lower end of the cost scale, while anything that involves building work going through the roof will be a lot more costly. If you are making changes in order to sell you should always consider what the market will tolerate. If local demand suggests that a two-bedroom semi has optimum saleability in a particular district there is little point adding another couple of bedrooms and expecting to recover your costs.

In terms of value increase, it would be fair to say that a good attic conversion will add slightly more to how much your property is worth than a basement conversion, due to the fact that most people simply prefer extra rooms on top rather than down below. As always, the costs of conversion must be set against the potential gain in real estate price. Remember, also, that nothing is ever as simple as it appears. An area that seems eminently ideal for conversion may throw up unforeseen problems, such as drainage, soil removal or roof-line issues. Local councils have become stricter over the past few years and it's now very difficult to get permission to do anything that interferes with the local skyline.

To ensure that your attic conversion is a valuable asset rather than a problematic burden, it can be worth employing an architect to draw up your plans. They'll be able to advise you on the logistics of your conversion,

▲ Loft conversions can make wonderful hideaways and the extra room can be a valuable addition to your home.

including where to put your windows and access staircases. And not only will you have their wealth of experience to tap into, but the plans will be helpful for both the planning authorities and your builder.

The same thinking applies to ground floor extensions and building above a garage, both of which can be good options if space allows.

Living on site or not?

Living on site is, in our experience, a completely different kettle of fish for every property. If works are minimal, being present at all times won't cause too much upheaval in your life. If you're about to start grand-scale redevelopment, however, being around all the time could become too much, particularly if you have young children. The most important consideration is whether you have alternative accommodation or not – six months in a rented property can add substantially to your costs. The ideal situation would be to keep your current property while the work continues on your new one, but beware: the loans required to maintain two addresses at one time can be crippling.

Extending down

In London at the moment anyone who is on the up-and-up is going down. Yup – astute city dwellers who're keen to get the most out of their square footage are looking at the option of heading down under in their quest for extra room. We all know about the value-adding benefits of a ground-floor extension at the back or side of the house, an extra room over the garage or a loft conversion but, when it comes to making the most of what lies beneath our property, we haven't even scraped the surface, *if* you'll excuse the pun. There are several options available, such as converting a cellar or digging below foundations to excavate an extra room, but each should be approached in the same way. First seek professional advice to see if your plans are structurally possible and then speak to your local planning authority. Planning consent, full surveys, specialist reports and structural appraisals will all be necessary, whatever you plan to do. Consents granted, this can be a wonderful opportunity to expand.

Legally, for a space to be a properly designated room it must have windows, adequate ventilation, decent access and a minimum ceiling height of 2 metres (7 feet) – check this figure with your local authority first. In short, all consents must be met. If you own your property freehold this means you also own the land on which the building stands. You will still need planning and building consents but you won't have to consult anyone else. But if you live in a ground-floor flat you will probably be a leaseholder and the freehold will be held by a landlord or shared with your neighbours upstairs (see Above and below on page 40 for options on buying them out). If you do manage to acquire the freehold it may still prove difficult to get approval for the works as the authorities might consider that the structural integrity of the whole building could be undermined. Either way, you'll need the help of experts – planners, architects and builders – to help you through the process.

A cellar or basement makes for the easiest conversion as the space already exists, although it may not always have windows. Forming windows below ground level means digging away at the side of the boundary wall, which may not be possible if, for example, the property is part of a terrace. The other option is to excavate at the front or rear of your property.

In terms of usage, we reckon the rooms best suited to life down under are kitchens, work rooms, bathrooms and studies. Bedrooms and living rooms are best located above ground level where daylight can flood in freely. But the choice, of course, is up to you.

Ascertaining potential capital value growth from your conversion is hard, but as a general rule rooms add value, anything from £30,000 to £50,000 according to the requirements of your area. Generally speaking there are returns to be had, but the costs of excavation can be as much, if not more, than simply extending, so do bear this in mind.

▼ Making the most of the area below your house can create extra living space both inside and outside. This not only adds value to your home but also improves quality of life.

Retrospective planning

These two simple words are enough to strike terror into even the most stoical individual. Fortunately, we've never had any real planning problems ourselves, but we've heard many tales of deceit and disaster in the big bad world of property development. So what's the deal? Well, retrospective planning does exactly what it says on the tin: it considers planning approval retrospectively – *after* the event. This is always bad news. We have come across several properties where changes have been made to original floor plans, or where extensions have been built or attics converted, without the official consents. We have always avoided them because things can get really complicated if you try to apply for retrospective planning permission. In theory, anybody who puts a property up for sale should tell the truth about changes that require retrospective planning or building consent. In reality, of course, buyers are often kept in ignorance. Local authority planning departments tend to look very unfavourably on alterations completed without their approval and they have the power to compel the owner – and that includes the new owner – to reinstate a property to its former condition. This can mean pulling down an extension, 'unbuilding' an attic conversion or even rebuilding something that has been demolished without a warrant. Heartbreaking – and costly. So always check before you buy.

DIY or project manager?

The letters DIY slide easily off the tongue these days, accustomed as we've all become to home improvement. If you're planning just to make small cosmetic changes to your property do-it-yourself really is your best, and cheapest, option. Less familiar, perhaps, is the term 'project manager'.

What a project manager might do for you

- The PM will help save costs by sourcing the best team and products for each part of the job.
- A good PM will use their site experience to make your project run smoothly.
- The PM will be your eyes and ears on site if you have to be absent.
- The PM will be accountable – though not to blame – should costs overrun.
- The PM should be able to answer every question you have pertaining to the ongoing work. If they can't, they'll know someone who can.

Previously employed by architects, professional builders, local councils and property development companies, project managers (PMs) make sure that all building work is done properly, on schedule and within budget. So if you're planning to make large, ambitious changes to your home a good PM really can save you a lot of time, trouble and money. Their experience should help smooth certain processes, such as guiding changes through planning or speaking to the best person at the local council. They will help you interpret your architect's plans (if relevant) and decipher any jargon you may be unsure about. Project managers will tend to be office-based and will spend their time securing the best quotes for every aspect of a job. They can work from inception to completion – or throughout whichever period you wish – and will charge you in one of three ways: a flat fee for the whole job, with payment to be made in stages; a weekly wage; or a percentage – perhaps 10% – based on the estimated cost of the entire project.

Hiring a project manager

1 From our experience of hiring PMs we favour the flat fee option, with the total figure and terms of payment agreed at the outset. Doing this means we know how much to set aside for the work and we are protected against escalating costs. A good PM should be happy enough to agree terms in this way. Be wary of the '10% of project cost' arrangement as this figure will rise if the estimated costs go up for any reason.

2 While the thought of employing a PM might seem daunting at first because of how much it will cost, you should appreciate that a good one can save you money in other areas. It is a basic function of a PM to negotiate discounted trade prices on all materials and to work out the most cost-effective way of carrying out all aspects of your building work.

3 Good PMs will not only save you money, they will also save you time – which, of course, means money in the end.

4 If you're employing an architect they should be able to put you in touch with a good PM. If you're not, try to find a PM through personal recommendations or, failing that, look in your local phone directory under 'Project Management Services' or 'Building Consultants'. Speak to several and ask about their experience to check it's relevant to your job. Ask for references and, as you would in any 'employing' situation, get all the facts and figures sorted out at the beginning of the project.

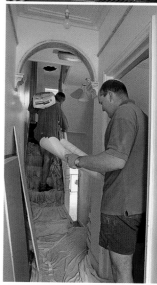

▲ If you can't be at your property to oversee the build every day, it's a good idea to hire a project manager.

Kitchens

The role of the previously humble, and indeed often overlooked, kitchen has changed dramatically over the last few decades. As styling inspirations broaden, we've learned to attach more importance to the space that has become, in many cases, the design-driven heart of our homes. No longer simply somewhere to prepare food or do the washing, the kitchen now presents itself as an opportunity to make a colossal lifestyle statement. When it comes to selling a house the kitchen is perhaps the most important room in the home, and you should always remember this.

So why is the kitchen so important?

A kitchen is very important as house buyers tend to take it as a yardstick for the rest of the house. Someone who sees a clean, well-planned kitchen will come away with the feeling that these qualities prevail throughout the property. Together with the bathroom, the kitchen is one of the few rooms that will be sold 'furnished as seen' – the flooring, sink unit, cabinets and maybe some of the appliances, such as the cooker, will be left behind for the new owners when you move. So always make sure your kitchen is meticulously maintained, beautiful and, as obvious as this might sound, *gleaming*.

Revamp or renew?

Whenever you buy a new property one of the most important decisions you make will be whether you should revamp or renew the existing kitchen. This decision, and the amount you spend, should be influenced by how you intend to use the property – whether you plan to live there or sell it straight away. Make sure you work out a budget before letting your imagination run wild, especially if you plan to employ a specialist designer. A gorgeous granite worktop may be the latest thing in kitchen style, but it will undoubtedly be expensive and limit your budget for the rest of the property. It's also not a guarantee of a good sale. The most important thing is to make the most of what you've got and, if necessary, renew one or two things, perhaps the floor or the units, so that the kitchen looks in good condition. While the fitted look is still popular, a less regimented style often works even better. In our opinion the best looks are those that are casual, comfortable and aspirational, but at the end of the day the room must simply 'work'.

▼ Make sure everthing you need in the kitchen is within easy reach. Appliances such as washing machines and dishwashers can be integrated so they're still accessible but don't spoil the design.

Layout, layout, layout

We're all using more appliances and gadgets in our kitchens these days so good basic design, especially of storage areas, is essential. We don't all have as much space in our kitchens as we would like but there are one or two things you can do to compensate. Narrow rooms, for example, tend to look better with eye-level units along only one wall and open shelving on the other, whereas bigger, squarer rooms can afford to be dressed along three walls. Try to avoid the 'boxed-in' effect created by having units on all four walls.

You are probably familiar with the concept of the 'work triangle', where the sink, fridge and cooker are placed so that they form an imaginary triangle. It's not a new idea, of course, but it's still a good working principle:

the sink, fridge and cooker are the three items used most often in a kitchen, so the idea is that you will save time and energy as you move from one to the other while preparing food and cooking.

The kitchen is always one of the most hard-wearing rooms in any property, but this is especially true if you're letting the house. Make sure the worktops and flooring are hardy and will stand the test of time – floor tiles and cork are sensible options. Neutral units and a simple layout are the key elements of a practical but stylish kitchen. If you're letting to design-conscious city slickers, make sure all the little details are of the highest quality.

> Buy to live – Create the kitchen you really want, but remember that one day you may decide to sell. Make up your mind whether your kitchen will be used for entertaining as well as cooking. Keep layouts clean and simple, ensure there are enough cabinets for storage and keep colour schemes easy. Whites and creams work well as do soft aqua shades like baby blue and turquoise. Shiny steel elements like splashbacks and worktops will give your kitchen a contemporary feel, or go for wooden cabinets if you prefer a 'country' look.
>
> Buy to sell – While attending to every last little design detail, don't forget who you're selling to. If the property is a one-bedroom bachelor pad you might want to install a breakfast bar, but for a family home a big table in the centre of the kitchen, if there's space, will seem welcoming as well as practical.

The importance of lighting

A good spread of light, both natural and electric, is very important in such a practical room as the kitchen. You will need strong, direct light in areas where you will be preparing and cooking food, but would probably prefer soft, diffused light in the dining area. Strip lighting fitted underneath wall cabinets is fine but can be harsh if used elsewhere. Unobtrusive lighting will add subtle mood and ambience to a room that could be austere or clinical, so go for wall sconces rather than ceiling pendants or globes.

Spotlights, too, can set the mood in the kitchen and can be used to highlight work zones and eating areas. A dramatic picture on one wall, to glam up the room, can be made even more attention-grabbing when picked out by a directional spot. There's no reason why you can't also use free-standing or floor lamps but, in our experience, the cables can get in the way and even prove dangerous in a room where 'trip hazards' are the last thing you need. If you do opt for this type of lighting make sure wiring is tucked out of harm's way.

Tips to make a tiny kitchen look bigger

- Don't be tempted by large, brightly coloured, free-standing fridges, freezers or cookers – choose smaller appliances in neutral colours and go for the fitted look to create a more streamlined effect.
- Don't try to put a table and four chairs in the kitchen if they end up looking cramped. Far from showing that there is room for a family to eat there you will end up drawing attention to the fact that it would not be a very comfortable experience for anyone. Instead, you could consider using a corner of the living room to create an intimate sit-down area, leaving the kitchen to speak for itself.
- Avoid dark colours as they can further diminish the available space. Opt instead for fresh light shades that allow light to 'bounce', creating a roomier feel.
- Keep eye lines clear and don't cram your worktops with unnecessary clutter. Pop all bits and pieces not currently in use out of sight in cabinets.
- Consider removing a couple of eye-level units and replacing them with chunky open shelving. You'll create the perfect place to show off your poshest ingredients and equipment!

◀ If you have a dual-function room, like a kitchen/diner, adopt one clear identity for both areas.

Five ways to make your kitchen look more expensive

1 Update your old units and make them look more expensive by fitting new door handles or knobs. DIY sheds and kitchen companies have a great range of handles that can be bought separately. Look for handles originally designed for wardrobes and sideboards as well, if you want something a bit different. Take inspiration from magazines or showrooms and then shop around to suit your budget – there's very little variation in quality these days, so don't feel you have to go for the designer name.

2 If you want to revitalize old timber cabinets or one of the many dated 'country cottage' DIY-store styles, consider a professional paint job. A specialist spray finisher (find one in the Yellow Pages or your local trade directory) will give an entirely new look to the most dilapidated of cabinets. It won't usually be necessary to have the cabinets sprayed all over, unless they're in a *really* bad state – opt instead for a recoat on drawer fronts and doors only. Expect to pay around £40 per door and £20 per drawer front. If you are feeling industrious or particularly budget-conscious you could do the job yourself. Opt for pale cream or eau de Nil for the Shaker look or a mid-blue for 'modern country'. To create a more industrial look you could go to a metal fabricator (again, grab your trusty Yellow Pages to find one), who should be able to measure and cut sections of 1-millimetre-thin stainless steel to your requirements. Simply fasten them in place with contact adhesive, available at most DIY stores. Doors can be updated in this way for around £30 each and, with the addition of a few chrome accessories, such as a kettle or a funky bread bin, you can achieve a very contemporary look.

3 Kick-boards (the strips that run below the doors on base cabinets) often look tired soonest, as do worktops, which take the brunt of day-to-day life. Replacing these will help provide a fresher look. Worktop lengths of 3 metres (10 feet) can cost from as little as £25 and, using a jigsaw (with your old worktop as a template), you can work wonders. Regrout any tiles (£10 kits readily available in DIY chains), polish the floor and clean all the windows. Every little helps!

▲ Details are as important in the kitchen as in the rest of the house. Chrome switches and taps and clever storage add to the room's appeal.

4 There are several 'mind game' ways to suggest your kitchen is newer or more expensive than it actually is. Imagine yourself, as a buyer, walking around it. If appliances such as the microwave, washing machine and cooker are up to date the suggestion is that this is a room where the budget

has been generous. At the point of sale, however, it will be up to you to decide if these are to be included or not. If you decide *not* to include them in the sale they can be used in your next house.

5 Pay attention to every detail, even the smaller ones such as taps and plug sockets. An attractive pillar tap can add new life to an old sink, and shiny chrome switches can give the impression of a much sharper finish throughout the room.

▲ Make sure surfaces stay as clear as possible to create a streamlined look.

Bathrooms

The importance of the bathroom can never be underestimated. It is often in this smallest room of the house that you can make the greatest impact. The state of your bathroom can make or break a sale, so invest a little time and effort here in order to 'clean up' in both senses of the term. Your family and guests will always appreciate having a haven to escape to, and so will any potential buyer. And if *you* don't love your own bathroom, how can you expect anyone else to?

A bathroom should refresh the person using it before a tap is even turned on, so that means creating a clean, fresh space that'll make your family, your guests and any potential buyers feel that they've just stepped into a health spa. Just like the kitchen, this is a room that is sold 'furnished as seen' so it's worth making sure it is equipped as well as you can possibly afford. A multisensory approach is crucial, so make your bathroom smell as sweet as it looks with scented candles and room sprays. Merchandising is also important and an Aveda bottle will say more than a Tesco's value-range bubble bath. If you can't afford the pick of your local perfumery's best decant less-expensive bath foams into stylish bottles and display them proudly. These days we all want sanctuary, reward and relaxation. Is your bathroom up to it?

Space solutions

As most bathrooms tend to be on the small side space is something you cannot afford to waste, so think about doubling up. Include tiled splashbacks that double as shelving, wall-mounted cabinets that free up floor space and a washbasin plinth that incorporates storage. Use light-reflective finishes like silk emulsion on the walls and choose shiny tiles and stainless-steel surfaces to bounce the available light around the room and increase the feeling of space. Mirrors are a must, so use them as splashbacks for a shower and vanity panels over the basin; or simply carve up any available plain walls with floor-to-ceiling mirrors to add an architectural touch and increase the perception of size.

Making the most of your bathroom may sound relatively easy compared to other home improvements (excavating basements, converting attics and adding conservatories, for example), but never underestimate the work involved. Should you decide to create a new bathroom in a space formerly occupied by a bedroom, for instance, you will need to ascertain whether it is already next to an existing plumbing track. If it isn't, the work involved is likely to be huge. You'll have to lift floorboards or chase the necessary pipe work up the walls and through the ceiling. You should seek professional

▲ Don't overcomplicate
your bathroom with
fussy decor – keep it
strong and simple.

advice on this and, once again, planning consents will be needed. If you want to create an en suite bathroom you'll have to call in the builders as well as the plumbers as you'll need a door and supporting joists. Be prepared!

Colour

Colour is the most important consideration in any room; after all, it has the strongest impact and is the easiest to change. Pale, pastel colours work especially well in bathrooms and can be used to increase the feeling of space. Consider painting three walls in one shade and the wall opposite the window or door in a lighter shade of the same colour to make the room appear larger than it is. Choosing a darker shade in a large bathroom can do the opposite, by bringing in a wall to create a cosier feel. Use cool aquatic blues, soft yellows and natural shades like calico and almond to conjure up a variety of different moods and to help maximize the light.

Equipment

Coloured bathroom suites are definitely out of fashion these days so always go for plain white sanitaryware – a straight-edged design is more sophisticated than shell-shapes or curves. A new white bath, basin and toilet is the perfect low-cost starting point and will allow you or a potential buyer to play around with colour in the rest of the room without spending a lot more money. Exotic tropical hardwoods such as wenge and iroko make attractive bath panels or washbasin splashbacks that will look both contemporary and indulgent, while stainless-steel and white tiles will help create a feel that is crisp and modern. Do use tropical hardwoods responsibly, however, and only buy from companies who can prove they import from sustainable forests.

Maximize the potential of your bathroom by installing a separate power shower if you have room or, if space is short, at least fit a stylish bath/shower mixer tap. Always give a potential buyer flexibility and the best you can afford. That way you will have an edge over the competition and you'll be one step closer to achieving a quick and profitable sale. Don't forget to research your market and dress your bathroom accordingly – chrome accessories will appeal to modernists while traditionalists will prefer the luxury of a gold finish. All the little extras will create a more attractive package for potential buyers – if we had a pound for every viewer who's asked 'Is that a power shower?' we'd be well on the way to making a fortune.

Buy to live – Create the room that you *really* want. Be indulgent and go for mini mosaic tiling, which never seems to date, or classic limestone flooring (see Case Study 4 on page 152). Muted colour schemes (natural or aqua) work best and refresh and enliven the room before you've even turned on a tap. If you need to invest in a suite make sure it's good-quality, for baths with scented candles, aromatherapy oils and a good book. As a general rule, white ceramics are best as colour schemes can be changed very easily by adding a splash of paint.

Buy to sell – Make the bathroom look as luxurious as possible. That doesn't mean dashing out to buy gold-plated taps, however, unless you are absolutely sure your potential buyers will be that way inclined! A quality white bathroom suite and shower are *so* much more important. Keep tiling simple, without pattern, so that you can appeal to the optimum number of people at all times. For the floor, opt for water-resistant laminates or good-quality, hard-wearing ceramics.

Lighting

Natural light is important in any room and the bathroom is no exception. It is a space dedicated to cleanliness, so it should be bright and welcoming and feel hygienic. Don't overdress the windows with fussy dust-trapping drapes; keep the look crisp and simple with blinds or frosted panels that let the light in while retaining privacy. If your bathroom doesn't have a window think of ways of introducing natural light with a skylight or internal fanlight windows with frosted glass. Failing that, there are various ways to be clever with lighting. A spread of sunken halogen spotlights in the ceiling can be very attractive and is a low-cost, stylish way of creating a pleasing effect. Use traditional or contemporary wall lights to frame mirrors and, for an even more dramatic impact, introduce back-lit frosted glass panels or set swimming-pool-style uplighters into the floor to pick out a particular zone. There is so much choice around these days, with prices to suit all budgets, that there's no excuse for not having a tastefully lit bathroom. One that is stylish and attractive could make all the difference to achieving your sale, so put in some effort and you'll really see the benefits.

Five ways to make your bathroom look more expensive

1 Mosaic tiles offer an affordable and stylish alternative to the traditional 152 × 152 millimetre (6 × 6 inch) bathroom tiles. Use more expensive coloured tiles sparingly as a border to increase visual impact.

2 Matching accessories like chrome toilet-roll holders, towel rails and wall-mounted soap dishes act like room jewellery and can add a sparkle to even the dullest bathroom.

3 Streamlining promotes a feeling of spaciousness, so panel in the toilet cistern and paint it to match the wall.

4 Taps make a huge difference – mix a budget white bathroom suite with more expensive taps to create a luxurious look.

5 Minimize clutter to maximize impact – clear away those messy shelves and make way for single larger items like vases and statues – the trick is to use these objects to create focal points and to display them in the way that an art gallery would show its best sculpture.

▶ In a limited space, minimum investment can provide maximum impact where flooring is concerned.

Flooring

For the single person or for a couple without a family, the prospect of padding around on a soft wool carpet after a bath or shower is extremely appealing, especially as you can now get water-repellent carpets that have been designed specifically for use in the bathroom. Add kids to the mix, however, and you soon realize that water-resistant floor coverings such as natural slate or ceramic tiles, Amtico or lino are best as they are hard-wearing and hygienic. Wood laminates are not a good idea as they need breathing space and do not react well to water, but there are some moisture-resistant varieties available so check with suppliers before buying. Cork is another option, but due to its potentially spongy nature, it will need to be sealed with several coats of varnish. The secret is to use a waterproof glue, and lots of it, so that the tiles never have the chance to curl up at the edges. As soon as that happens water will get underneath and you could be setting yourself all sorts of problems – mildew or, worse, damp.

Dark colours tend to make a room look smaller so go for light shades for your floor covering if space is limited. A cluttered bathroom can be very off-putting – always keep things off the floor and clear of the skirting boards to make the room look clean and spacious.

Heating

Heating in a bathroom should be functional and discreet – opt for small wall-mounted heaters, chrome radiators or underfloor systems depending, obviously, on the style of your home. Heated towel ladders are not only a great way to warm a bathroom, they also give you somewhere to hang your tastefully colour-coordinated towels. As well as being chic, they can now be bought from DIY stores for less than £100.

Storage and shelving

Open shelving is a good way to store and display bathroom products. Gorgeously packaged lotions and colour-coordinated towels add to the 'theatre' of a bathroom, but for medical items think clever mirror-fronted storage (two functions for the price of one) and anything that is beautiful as well as functional. DIY chains, high street stores and designer outlets all have good product ranges. Don't forget to include storage for medicines, etc. if you're renovating for selling – it's crucial to cover every issue that might concern a potential buyer.

Hallways and entrances

A hallway is the first thing your visitors see as they walk across your threshold. What impression do they get? Are you sending out the wrong signals? Is your hallway cluttered with bicycles, coats, outdoor shoes and a mountain of unopened post and free advertising literature? Well, get tidying! Just as it's crucial that the exterior of your home sets the scene for what lies inside, so too is it important that the first area any visitors see as they walk across your threshold – in most cases the hallway or stairs – is as good as it can possibly be. Judgements are made in an instant, and if you make mistakes at this initial stage it will be harder to convince buyers later – in our opinion, most buying decisions are made within the first 30 seconds of walking into a property, so don't mess up. The first impression should be of a welcoming home, regardless of whether your visitors are friends or potential buyers.

▼ First impressions count – increase the feeling of space in your hallway by clever use of mirrors.

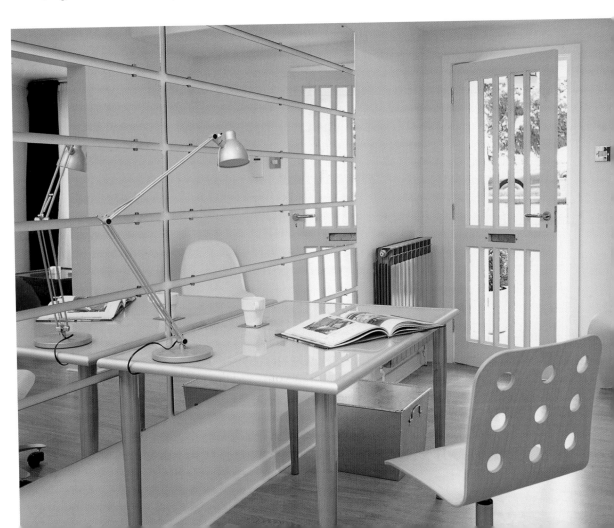

Buy to live – The key point is to make your hallway as comfortable and welcoming as you can. Invest in good-quality flooring that's beautiful but also practical. If you have a young family avoid lighter coloured carpets (think of the mud and those messy spillages!) and make sure your flooring is wipe-clean. Timber laminate floors, ceramic tiling and the new breed of flexible floors, such as Amtico, are durable and attractive and most are treated with stain repellents. In general, the more you pay the better the quality will be. Carpets or natural-weave floor coverings like jute or seagrass are a tactile feast; the last two are particularly hard-wearing. Opt for neutral colours on the walls; they won't date and will be easy to decorate around.

Buy to sell – Replacing the flooring in your hallway can give it a new lease of life. You can often get a great look from a budget carpet, which will create a good impression in the short term. There's no point shelling out £40 a square metre if a perfectly acceptable £10 a metre carpet could do the trick.

Wider entrance hallways

If you are fortunate enough to have a big hall there are a number of ways in which to make *big* statements as visitors arrive. A huge gold-framed mirror against a plain white wall will add grandeur to even the most modern environment. An arrangement of interesting pictures and prints will provide an almost gallery-like feel and will tempt prospective buyers to linger a little longer before moving into other areas of the home.

We once had a client in Brighton, with a very limited budget, who commissioned us to design a streamlined kitchen and to create a space for dining in an already compact living room. This was going to be difficult. Then we took a look at his hallway, which was a rectangular space of some 3 × 4 metres (10 × 14 feet) and we knew we had found the ideal solution. With his kitchen and bathroom accessed from a second inner hallway with separate doors, there were no planning consent problems to get in our way. We simply redecorated the main hallway in natural shades and suggested a range of dark-wood dining furniture to complement the natural seagrass flooring we had chosen. The finishing touch was the concealed lighting set into the cornice, which created the impression that the ceiling was much higher than it actually was. A bit of lateral thinking had led to a strikingly simple but effective solution – often it's just a matter of making the most of what's already there.

Points to consider

1 Maximize the feeling of space. If your hallway is particularly narrow choose pale colours to make it look wider. A typical British home will often have a hallway that is disproportionately tall in relation to its width, and if this is the case in yours there are certain things you can do to counteract this. Using a shade several tones darker than the main wall colour from the picture-rail up will help to make the ceiling seem lower and the whole space appear wider. If you have a long straight corridor leading from the front door to the back of the house create a foreshortened effect by painting the far wall in a darker, or more distinctly contrasting, colour than the main walls.

2 Brighten up a dull and dingy hallway with clever lighting. Sometimes all you need to do is increase the wattage of the bulbs you use in your ceiling lights, but if you want to try something more radical consider halogen spotlights or track lighting. The individual spots can be directed to light up those difficult corners that simple pendant lights cannot reach. If you want to create more of a mood or ambience in your hallway don't forget that side lighting and table lamps can be very effective.

3 Resist using the hallway as a dumping ground for items you don't want to store in other rooms – your hallway should look inviting. Give visitors something to stop and admire instead of giving the impression that this is simply a functional passageway leading to other, more exciting parts of your home. Do you have room for a slim console? If not, at least put an attractive mirror on the wall. Add a couple of candlestick lamps and some pictures to create a space that sets the tone for the rest of your home.

Stairs and landings

The same decorating principles that apply elsewhere should be applied to stairways and landings. Instead of treating them as simple passageways that get you from A to B, try to see them as an integral part of the overall design in your home. One look that works particularly well in older properties is a painted staircase with carpets or floor runners held in place with chrome or brass stair-rods.

▶ Turn dead space into living space. Here, a windowless inner hallway has been transformed into a comfortable dining room.

Flooring

If you want to achieve an all-in cohesive look that will make a favourable impression, use the same carpet in the main hallway and on the landings and upstairs corridors. As well as looking luxurious and adding colour, carpets help to deaden the echoes that can sometimes make hallways and passages seem cold and draughty. But if you are lucky enough to have a property with its original floors still in place – flagstones, oak floorboards, decorative tiling or inlaid mosaics, for example – don't cover them up, but be proud of them and show them off. It is amazing how much value these original period features can add to your home. If you really can't tolerate the totally bare look in your hallway put a rug down to soften the effect, but make sure all your visitors can see and admire a floor that could make your property unique.

▲ LEFT: Make sure your choice of colour scheme in the hallway complements that of the adjoining rooms. RIGHT: As with all features, if you've got an attractive staircase, let it speak for itself. Here, an open staircase allows natural light to filter down to the lower hallway.

Five ways to make your hallway look more expensive

1 In darker hallways, if character and style allow, consider replacing a solid front door with one that has glass inserts.

2 In many modern properties, particularly those built between 1950 and 1980, you are likely to find plain doors made out of sapele, an African hardwood that is similar to mahogany but nowhere near as beautiful. Sapele doors are a dull reddish-brown with absolutely no character, and they are *everywhere*. If you don't want to replace them there are a couple of things you can do to make them less boring. You could add panelling, which would make them look older and more traditional, or you could paint them. If you have these doors in rooms leading off your hallway you will reduce their impact if you paint all of them the same colour as the walls. This will also make your hallway look bigger.

3 Banish all clutter. The average hallway is not big enough for everyone's coats and shoes, so get rid of them. A hefty clump of clothes will take up valuable space in your passageway, so banish those macs and wellingtons. If you haven't got space for them elsewhere, try creating an alcove under the stairs and fixing pegs on the wall to carry the coats. If there's room, stick a table in front to distract the eye.

4 If there is enough room for an occasional table or a comfy chair, try to establish a convincing living zone in your hallway. Even if you don't spend any time there yourself it will give people the impression that it is a usable space that many other homes don't have. However, if your hallway really is small don't cram it with furniture as you'll only draw attention to the space's limitations.

5 Improve eye lines by boxing in any electricity or gas meters that are traditionally housed in hallways. There is no way of making them look pretty, so hide them away in a neat, streamlined timber-fronted unit painted to blend in with the surrounding décor. You could also box in any exposed pipes.

Living areas

Living rooms should do *exactly* what their name suggests and be comfortable rooms for living in. Whether in a family house or a couple's flat, the living room will be the hub of many central home functions, such as relaxing, eating, working and watching TV. Although the kitchen is often considered to be the heart of the home, for most people, the main living area is the one with the most allure. Look at your own home situation – where do *you* spend your free time?

Getting your living space just right

Tailoring your living area to meet your requirements is essential for a comfortable home life. This could be as simple as adding a phone line for an internet connection, or as colossal as knocking down walls to create an open plan living/dining/kitchen space. The main consideration is creating a space that is right for you. If you have a large family or like to entertain lots of friends, then ample seating will be a priority, with easy access from the dining/kitchen areas even more desirable if you like to cook for them, too. Don't rush into any grand plan, however, without thinking through every detail first. It could be that your current abode is perfectly laid out already – if it ain't broke, why fix it?!

Creating a comfortable scene

We all have different expectations regarding what we want from every room in our home, but we place the most demands on the living area. It should be an inviting space, giving off a sense of calm and order, but it also has to be practical and comfortable. While we pass roughly a third of our lives in the bedroom, we're usually asleep, whereas in the living area, we're awake and ready to relax. You should make the space as indulgent as you can by choosing wonderful furniture to suit your own taste or your potential market. Try to appeal to all the senses – layer sofas with comfortable throws and cushions and make sure the lighting is adjustable and directional. The space should feel like a cosy sanctuary, hidden from the pressures of the outside world.

When planning your living area think about what it will be used for, apart from lounging. Will it have to accommodate a dining table? Will it have to double as a study? Take these and other factors into consideration and you'll create a space that will enhance your life rather than hinder it.

Allow for ample space to accommodate your TV and hi-fi paraphernalia. And if the hub of the outside world is right outside your window, you may need double glazing to give you peace and quiet.

▲ Get the balance right – use equal measures of comfortable seating and stylish accessories to create the perfect interior.

Colour-scheming

The colours you choose to decorate with will either add to or distract from the character of your space. So if you're looking to market your home, it makes sense to keep colour scheming muted so that prospective buyers are not distracted from the matter in hand by unusual shades chosen by you in a moment of colour-charged folly. Vivid orange, lime green or electric blue may be your favourite colours, but they will not do you any favours in your Edwardian semi when it comes to tempting a sale. Best advice, as always, is to know your market. Why not ask your estate agent what works best, in colour terms, in your specific area? Bear in mind that a cool English urbanite buying in London's up-and-coming East End might hope that his or her Victorian terrace is finished in a completely different style to an older couple buying a similar property in Dundee.

Of course, whether you're selling on or planning to live in the property for some time, cohesion is paramount with all colour schemes. If your living space has multiple purposes, for example cooking and dining as well as relaxing, working and entertaining, think about the space as one and colour it accordingly. If you've used lots of blond wood furnishings in the seating area, employ similar timber styles for dining furniture and kitchen units. Colour on walls can be used to delineate between different functions, but try to stay close in tone to other colours used.

▲ Exposing original features will enhance the appeal of your home. Fireplaces in particular will provide a focal point to help tie your look together.

Flooring

If your living room is destined to be the main 'gathering' room, then wear and tear is likely to be the main consideration when it comes to choosing flooring, particularly in a family house. Laminate floors are extremely hard wearing and, due to high consumer demand, their price has dropped in recent years. Available in an increasing range of wood colours and finishes, there's sure to be something to suit every taste and budget. On the negative side, however, there's little noisier than a hoard of kids charging across a laminate floor so, if you're living in a flat, do consider your neighbours.

> **Buy to live** – Form over function might be a popular saying in interior design terms, but in everyday life the opposite actually applies. That modular linear sofa may look droolsomely gorgeous in your local interiors store, but will it be ergonomic enough to satisfy the needs of a busy family? In simpler terms, will it be comfy as well as gorgeous? And don't be tempted to follow fashions – pick a neutral decor and add colour through soft furnishings and accessories.
>
> **Buy to sell** – Put the room together so that it 'applies' to the relevant market. Without wishing to generalize, if you're likely to be selling to a cool young bachelor there's little point in decking out the space with florals and patterns. Muted colours are always better than bright as they allow the viewer to imagine their own personality imposed on the surroundings. And don't overcrowd the room with furniture you don't need – the most important commodity of any home is space, so pare down and open up.

If you have an older property, there may be a wooden floor lurking under the carpet. If it's in good condition, why not think about sanding the boards and staining them to bring out the beauty of the wood? An original feature like this can add value to your home and is always popular with potential buyers.

Don't forget the cosy feel of soft carpet underfoot. Choose wisely, however, if you take this option, as there's nothing worse (and more off-putting to potential buyers) than a busily patterned carpet cluttering up a room. Go for plain colours or opt for one of the natural weaves, like sisal, seagrass and coir.

Fireplaces

Fireplaces add focus to a room as well as a sense of warmth and cosiness. Use the fireplace as a starting point to decide where to position furniture and how to decorate. An original fireplace will look wonderful once restored – don't remove it unless you absolutely have to.

Living flame gas fires are popular, as they have the look and feel of a real fire without all the hard work. Try and let your fire surround speak for itself and choose as simple a gas fire as possible – some of the glitzier options available could detract from the surround and date the overall look of your room.

If you fancy a real fire, do consider the work involved – cleaning, lighting, carrying coal/logs, etc. If you're not put off, then employ a chimney sweep to remove any blockages that could catch fire. Finally, choose your fuel. In some areas (especially towns and cities), you have to use smokeless fuel to avoid pollution – check with your local council's environmental services department.

Creating focus

If your living area lacks a focal point you should create one. And it should be one that is worth looking at – how many times have you walked into a room to find that the TV set is the first thing you see? A chimney breast is usually the most obvious feature to draw the eye in. Paint it in a contrasting shade to the other walls to bring it into focus. If there's no hearth, you can create the illusion of one with a floating shelf on the wall at mantelpiece height and a painted black square below. A mirror above the shelf and an artistic arrangement of logs or pebbles in a wicker basket on the floor will complete the effect.

Another way to create a focal point is to use a painting or sculpture. Even a cleverly placed console and some symmetrically positioned ceramics, or an arrangement of unusual house plants, will give the room the direction it needs.

▼ Living rooms should have room to live, so don't overstuff them with furniture. Leave clear eyelines to maximize the space and promote the comfort factor.

▲ LEFT: Breathe life into an unused corner of your home by adding comfortable furniture and a splash of colour. RIGHT: Spark your imagination with an unusual modern take on a traditional log fire.

Lighting

The key to successful lighting in any room is control and that means being able to adjust illumination levels to create a variety of moods and uses. This might sound rather technical and complicated, but actually boils down to very simple ideas, such as dimmer switches on overhead lighting and standard and table lamps dotted around the room.

Occasional lighting allows you to create 'mood pools' that can make a space more cosy or focus on a dramatic mirror or piece of artwork. High street stores now have more lighting ranges than you can possibly imagine, and you'll easily be able to find traditional and enduringly popular designs alongside more modern innovations.

Storage and shelving

Storage is vital in your living area. Think about what you'll be using the room for – if it's for reading, then you'll need bookshelves, and if it's for watching TV and listening to music, then you'll need somewhere for all those CDS, videos, DVDs and technological paraphenalia. Storage should be discreet, blending into the room rather than standing out. Doors are essential for hiding clutter away; open shelving may seem like a great idea, but is best used for displaying smaller items. Built-in storage can look fantastic, but can be quite expensive, as you'll most likely have to employ a carpenter.

As with all storage, don't let it dominate the space, otherwise you'll feel like you're sitting in a warehouse. And make sure everything you've stored away is close to where it will be used to make life as easy as possible.

Studies and workspaces

How many of us now share our homes with personal computers and fax machines? The problem is, most houses were not designed to accommodate this new technology. Look around – where do you keep your PC? Is it monopolizing the dining table, balanced precariously at one end of the breakfast bar, sitting on a wobbly shelf or desk in a child's bedroom, or banished to a depressing spare room where it is surrounded by household junk and clutter? *Exactly*. Modern house-builders are cottoning on to the fact that a lot of people now work from home, so they are sacrificing the traditional third or fourth bedroom in favour of a dedicated office space. If a separate work or study zone is important for you it should be designed with as much care and attention as any other room in the house.

If your life demands somewhere to work, consider this when viewing a property or planning how to develop it. If you're selling in a professional area somewhere to work is vitally important. If possible, include creating this space in your plans from the start to avoid adapting a room, at extra cost, once you've done all the other work. There doesn't have to be a whole room dedicated to the home office – sometimes the space under the stairs will do just fine. Wherever it is, make sure your PC set-up is tidy, user friendly and in harmony with its surroundings. After all, be it for business or pleasure, your computer must be placed in such a way as to allow it to perform fully without hampering the functions of any other home activities.

Make sure you have enough power points and that they are close to the area where you plan to install your workstation or desk. Nothing spoils the look of a well-managed study more than a Spaghetti Junction of cables and wires cluttering up the streamlined space. Advances in wireless infrared technology will soon, we hope, see the end of these messy cable connections and should allow for greater flexibility as far as the positioning of computers is concerned. In the meantime, there are several types of flexible tube that are designed specially to accommodate cables, so hit your nearest computer store.

Setting up your office

There are many things to consider when you're planning an office or workspace, from storage to colour-scheming, from layout to lighting. If you are able to dedicate an entire room to a home office, plan everything from the start so that you end up with the most efficient and productive use of space – don't forget that computers often come with a lot of other equipment. Comfort is extremely important, so it's worth investing in a supportive office

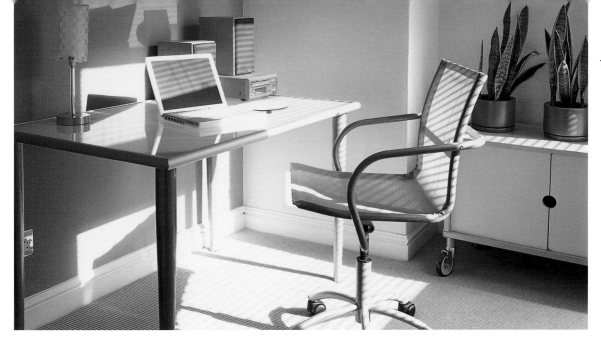

chair rather than pulling up a stool. Ergonomics should be taken into account when buying a desk – think of available workspace, desk height and drawer capacity and look carefully at how a curved desk edge could facilitate a more comfortable working position. Consider installing a second phone line, so that whoever is using the computer doesn't cause a breakdown in communications for anyone else living under the same roof.

Avoid placing your computer in direct sunlight, but do make use of any natural light as the main light source. Blinds at the windows, instead of curtains, will create a more businesslike and streamlined appearance.

▲ In a small office, keep inclusions and clutter to a minimum. A simple desk, a chair and some sleek storage should be all you need.

Storage

Storage is also paramount – consider units with doors that close so that you can hide some of the clutter that inevitably accumulates in any office. There's nothing more distracting than having piles of paperwork on your desk, staring back at you when you're trying to concentrate on something else. Getting the storage furniture right is about so much more than simply rushing out and buying a couple of filing cabinets and a new set of shelves. Clever buying will make the space function at its optimum level. Think dual purpose – desks with extra drawers built in, wall cabinets that double up as stationery stores and lighting that is good for both mood and direction. These days there is no excuse for creating austere and uninviting spaces – high street stores have really responded to the needs of the home-office user. Many now carry exciting furniture ranges that will look perfectly at home in a domestic environment. Modern, sleek storage design suggests slick professionalism and, even if it's only you who will see it, it will do your psyche and output a power of good if a sense of order and aesthetic pleasure prevails. Throw a potential buyer into the mix and it will really promote you and your home.

Lighting

One of the most important things to remember when planning your workspace is that light levels should be spread evenly around the room. Dimmer-controlled lights are excellent as they can be adjusted when more or less light is required. Make sure there are no strong sources of light that could glare on your monitor screen and cause headaches, although a desk lamp can be a good idea if you're going to be working late into the night.

Heating

Government health and safety guidelines cover temperatures and ventilation in the work place and you too should think about these things. Create a work-friendly atmosphere in your home office by making sure it is warm in winter, cool in summer and always well ventilated. If you are going to sit at a computer for long periods invest in a room humidifier, ionizer or electric fan to avoid fatigue and dry eyes and skin.

▼ Satisfy demand – if you think your potential buyer may need office space, provide precisely that by creating the perfect home work zone.

Buy to live – Because very few homes are designed with technology in mind, it's important to create an office that can house all the gadgets and computer equipment you need, but in a neat, tidy and efficient way. Think of installing phone links, internet connections and extra power requirements at the planning stage, to ensure the finished space is streamlined. Avoid strong, distracting colours – soft, natural shades will evoke a good working atmosphere.

Buy to sell – Keep the office organized – a workspace should be orderly and efficient, so invest in stylish storage systems to keep clutter at bay. Don't go overboard with wall-to-wall built-in shelving – it's not attractive and potential buyers need rooms to be as flexible as possible.

Fitting in

If you don't have the luxury of a separate room that you can set aside for a home office or study at least try to make sure you have somewhere permanent for your computer to live, and that it relates sympathetically to the rest of the room. For example, if you have put your PC in the dining room you could house it in a ventilated armoire-style cabinet and tidy it away by simply closing the door.

Doubling up with other home functions is another great way to achieve invisible 'stealth' technology at home. Think of internet-ready televisions or DVD-drive PCs that allow computer functions to be viewed through normal televisions so that there's no need for separate monitors. This basic move towards 'collaborative technology' will save you loads of valuable space.

The power of suggestion

Subliminal signalling is always a great secret weapon when it comes to marketing your home. As far as we are concerned the domestic office set-up says a lot about you – and consequently your home – as buyers wander around. Everybody wants to be successful, and the appearance of working from home and being your own boss can shout achievement, attainment and fulfilment. So even if you don't use your PC very often make sure it's set up in its own area so that viewers can see there is a designated space for working at home. A proper workspace will reflect a lifestyle that many people will perceive as desirable and they'll project themselves into your environment. It could be the key to a profitable sale.

Bedrooms

The biggest room in your home is the room for improvement. When you are selling, every room should captivate a prospective buyer. It's not uncommon, though, for people to concentrate on the public areas of their homes – the entrance hall, the living areas and the kitchen – and neglect the bedrooms because they see these as private areas. Our advice is: don't. There should be no afterthoughts; no second, third or fourth bedrooms. All bedrooms are equal, so treat them all with the same level of respect. Is your spare bedroom undecorated and unloved, filled with clutter that you never touch? You may have no problem with this when you're the only person who sees the room, but it's not a good idea when you've got people coming to look around.

Space solutions

A bedroom – any bedroom – should be a restful, clutter-free area. If you are overwhelmed with 'stuff' start decluttering and spring-cleaning now. If possible, don't have your office or study zone in your bedroom because subconsciously your workload will nag at you when you should be relaxing and sleeping. There should be no distractions in a bedroom – sleep and regeneration are too important. Ideally, you want to rise each morning to clean and tidy surroundings, well equipped to face the day. Have only the things you really love in your bedroom and keep the emphasis on comfort and beauty. With this in mind storage is an issue that must be addressed. If you need help turning your nightly nightmare into a real dream scenario, follow the tips on page 106.

Lighting

Lighting, as ever, is important and should be flexible enough to cover every occasion. Dimmer switches are inexpensive and are great for changing the mood. What's more, they now come in a variety of finishes to satisfy your particular style requirements – chrome, brass or even wood. Built-in wall lighting or overhead spotlighting doesn't cost a lot but can look incredibly sophisticated. As usual, remember to plan for this type of lighting at the start of your building work to allow for wiring and replastering.

Think about putting halogen downlights in the ceiling to illuminate the space evenly without creating any dark areas. Use matching lamps on bedside tables placed on either side of a double bed or opt for two lamps on a console table placed directly under a picture on the wall. Pairing lights in this way will give the picture added drama and make it the focal point of the room.

▲ Sweet dreams are made of this: space, textures and clean lines – all the components required for a good night's sleep.

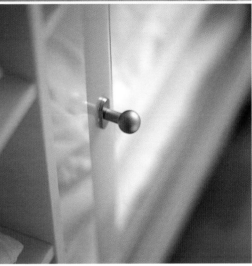

Buy to live – When planning your ideal bedroom consider what you will need the room for – sleeping, dressing, reading, watching television – and plan your space accordingly. Tailor the room to your specific requirements (there's no point having a huge walk-in wardrobe if you've no interest in fashion).

Buy to sell – Make space as flexible as possible to facilitate a variety of uses. The bedroom should be restful, calming and aesthetically pleasing, so opt for neutral palettes or add colour and identity using bold artwork. Fitted carpets are a must – you can get the look of expensive flooring with cheaper alternatives if you shop around. Don't worry if your bed is a standard divan rather than antique French – if it's well dressed it will sell the bedroom. High street stores, such as TXMaxx, offer quality bedding ranges at vastly reduced prices. Pile up the pillows, layer the throws and fold back those crisp white sheets.

Five ways to declutter your bedroom

1 Lose those bulging wardrobes by sorting through your clothes. Be ruthless and get rid of anything you don't wear any more. A trip to the local charity store will help *everyone*. Seasonal adjustment is another way to save space, so put your winter wardrobe into storage during the summer months and vice versa.

2 Divan storage is a great way to use the space under the bed – although this is not recommended if you're into feng shui as clutter under beds is believed to block sleep energy. Clever firms like the Holding Company produce stylish wheeled storage boxes that are specially made to go under beds with legs.

3 If you have an old chest of drawers that you no longer need, pop castors on the base of each drawer to create a simple storage system that will slide neatly under your bed.

4 Invest in some stylish boxes to contain and replace the clutter usually found on top of wardrobes.

5 Tuck an unsightly TV set into a cabinet that you can close when you're not watching television.

▶ Don't commit a spare bedroom exclusively to guests. By dressing a divan bed as a sofa and adding a comfy chair, you can create a room for living as well as sleeping.

Colour

A soft, soothing, sophisticated sanctuary – that's what a bedroom should appear to be, so choose your colours carefully. Soft whites with a hint of a tint will give you a generous palette of non-aggressive colours that will allow you to introduce a stronger element of each 'hinted at' colour to provide identity and maybe a touch of drama. Chalky pastels are easy living and look amazing teamed with stronger masculine colours like grey and brown. Reds, black and gold are flirty, sexy and downright dangerous! Texture is the new colour, especially in the bedroom, so go for contrasts like satin sheets with mohair throws or sheer muslin bed-drapes with warm wool blankets – gorgeous.

Flooring

Warmth is an important consideration in the bedroom so think of padding about on soft wool carpets or on giant island rugs adrift on a sea of sanded floorboards. Try to avoid busy patterned carpets or rugs in favour of tone-on-tone flooring: it will be more soothing and rewarding to the eye. Natural wool carpets are best for feel appeal, but if you can't quite stretch to those pick one of the cheaper man-made fibre/wool mixes for a similar look.

Laminate flooring is sleek and very popular, but avoid the clinical office look by opting for a soft graining that echoes the beauty of real wood.

Built-in wardrobes

Built-in wardrobes should be just that, so make sure they don't look like afterthoughts and that they fit the overall scheme. Extend existing wall coving across the wardrobe fronts to blend them in further, or ensure that your wardrobe matches the wall colour to disguise where the wall finishes and the wardrobe begins. Built-in wardrobes are a plus when it comes to selling, but try to avoid mirrored ones – they're not as fashionable as they once were.

Furniture

You can't have a great bedroom without having a great bed, so don't be afraid to splash out a little. You spend one-third of your life in bed so don't skimp on the quality of the mattress. And don't forget just how big a bed can be – measure room sizes before buying and leave enough clearance space all round. Before buying the latest 'designer' bed consider the cost-effective option of choosing a simple classic divan that you can update and adapt with new bedlinen. A change of bedding equals a change of colour scheme, so think of a palette you can mix and match to satisfy a variety of moods. You can disguise a cheaper bed with plain bedding sculpturally dressed with colour-coordinated throws and pillows. Add luxurious elements like suede, cashmere and silk to boost the glamour.

Storage and shelving

Storage is a crucial consideration when planning your bedroom. Leave enough space to accommodate wardrobes, drawer units and shelves as well as the bed and think of ways of doubling up – an armoire that houses a hi-fi as well as your clothes, for example, or a dresser that cleverly doubles as a blanket box. If your budget is limited, opt for a range from B&Q or Ikea and add extra shelving, tie racks and mirrors to make it look more expensive.

Heating

Visible heating is the ultimate in bedroom luxury. Open fires provide a visual and very tangible warmth and are therefore incredibly inviting. Time-controlled heating will give you cool conditions overnight and warmth when you wake in the morning. Underfloor heating is ideal for those who love to pad about barefoot, and as this option is becoming cheaper and easier to run than it used to be you can now push the luxury factor to the max for the minimum cost.

Think style and functionality and go for a heating system that will satisfy both criteria. Refurbished old school radiators are fun and funky, while companies like Bisque produce heating that is sculptural as well as practical.

Other bedrooms

These design principles are the same for every bedroom, but for children's, teenagers' and guest bedrooms, there are a few other things to consider. In children's rooms, the priority is closed storage so that toys can be tidied away. But do allow space for some of their belongings to be on display. Teenagers will probably be using their bedrooms for living, dining and entertaining as well as sleeping, so go for comfort and flexibility above all else – and if you're brave enough, let them have a free hand in the design and layout.

Guest bedrooms should be treated like master bedrooms and lavished accordingly. Self sufficiency is a good idea so, if space allows, plan for en suite facilities, wardrobes and possibly even a television.

▲ Dedicated under-bed storage is a clever way of keeping your bedroom clutter-free.

Five ways to make your bedroom look more expensive

1 If you don't have the luxury of a dedicated dressing room consider built-in wardrobes. They suggest order, streamlining and care but they can also dominate a room, so only use them where there is enough floor space.

2 Add an 'area' rug as a colourful marker to delineate space and help you to pull all your colours together. It can add a comfortable warm touch and may be the only pattern, colour or design you'll need.

3 Mix the old and the new. Square boxy-shaped bedheads look great with ornate antique gilt mirrors to create a modernist take on hot hotel style.

4 For a luxurious, romantic look dress the windows with fabrics that flow, billow or look good built up in layers. For a more modern feel go for blinds. Either way, when it's time for 'lights out' make sure your curtains or blinds will give you total blackout to aid unbroken, restful sleep.

5 Symmetry works well in a bedroom, so pair off bedside tables, lamps and easy chairs. Designers like to group three objects of a similar type together but in the bedroom two's company and three's most definitely a crowd.

▼ Create the ultimate comfort zone with thick indulgent layers of silky bedding, fluffy throws and touchy-feely cushions.

The great outdoors

One of the most important and bankable characteristics of any property is how much usable space it offers or, in other words, the number of rooms it has. Anything you can do to maximize this will be rewarded when the time comes to sell. When you've done all you can do indoors why not turn your attention to the great outdoors? Have you thought about adding a conservatory, a dedicated patio area or even a balcony? We are all now beginning to see a garden as an extra room, so giving it a practical function rather than just a decorative look is another way of adding value to your home. Extensions don't just work on the living space, they work on bank balances too!

How do you want to use your outside space?

It is one of the most overused sentences in garden design, but nevertheless it is good advice – treat your garden like another room in your house and give it a use and an identity. Are you stuck for living space in a tiny house with a huge garden? Well, amend the balance and you'll reap the rewards accordingly, both personally and financially.

▼ Conservatories are a great way of bringing the outside in, but make sure the space that borders your garden and your home is at one with both.

Think carefully about what you plan to do with any available space – you don't want to build a huge extension and leave yourself with no garden at all. If you're short on space, think about creating a patio area linked to the house with large French windows. Accessorizing with outdoor furnishings of a similar style to those that you have indoors will complement the interior and extend the feeling of space and continuity.

Conservatories

Conservatories, sun lounges, garden rooms – call them what you will, they're a great way of adding usable space to your house. They are useful design tools too, providing a connection between the indoor and the outdoor worlds. Of all the possible building extensions, there is something tangibly pleasurable about being in a conservatory and being able to enjoy the garden whatever the weather. But before you start knocking down the back walls and laying the foundations ask yourself what you will use your new conservatory for: an additional living room, a dining room, a children's play area, a place to grow plants? And remember, even a self-build conservatory will require proper foundations to counteract damp and drainage problems, so you'll probably need to call the builders in, unless you're a DIY champion.

Planning

If your planned conservatory is less than 70 cubic metres (247 cubic feet), is situated at the back of the house and has a glass or translucent roof you shouldn't need planning permission. If, on the other hand, you're planning something a bit grander, or if your house is listed or in a conservation area, it's more than likely that you will need to get planning permission. If you have any doubts or questions consult your local council's planning department. Whatever you do, don't rely on friends and neighbours for advice, and don't necessarily rely on the company you choose to build the conservatory to bring you up to speed on consents. Check it all out yourself, do everything legally and you'll save yourself a truckload of hassle. (See Retrospective planning on page 74).

Sympathetic, stylish and spacious

Sympathetic, stylish and spacious: these are the three main qualities to look for in any area of home improvement, and your conservatory is no exception. Make sure the new extension complements your home – you don't want to end up with a white carbuncle plonked onto the front of your Palladian mansion! Always spend as much as you can afford on a quality conservatory and avoid building anything that is more plastic than glass. If budget allows, opt for a hardwood or modern UPVC conservatory that is simple and unfussy. Avoid softwood frames and single glazing as they will provide you with little or no insulation and soundproofing. What's more, they'll age quickly and will not withstand the elements well. Polycarbonate roofs are difficult to keep clean and tend to look cheap, so try and stretch that extra length and invest in toughened glass.

If you can't decide on the type of conservatory to choose, take a walk around your neighbourhood. What have other people done? If you see something you like don't be afraid to knock on the door and find out who built the conservatory and how much it cost. Contact the National Conservatory Advisory Council (NCAC) for advice on styles, materials, dimensions, planning permissions and constraints. They also have a register of approved conservatory builders, so they can help you to find a reputable company in your area and avoid the cowboys.

Another reason for checking out the properties in your area that have conservatories is to see how much they are selling for. This will give you some idea of how much you should spend. After all, there's no point in paying out for a £30,000 extension for your £60,000 house if the neighbouring properties with conservatories are only selling for £70,000. You don't always get back what you put in, so think about potential profit margins *before* you spend and then adjust your budget accordingly.

Extra features mean extra profits

Once you've shelled out and built your conservatory you need to decide how to make it feel special and so add even more value to your home. Think about extra features like access doors to the garden, a ventilation/air-conditioning system and, of course, attractive blinds so that you can control the amount of light coming in. Heating is another important consideration as it will make an all-year-round space. The same continuous flooring between the conservatory and the adjoining room will elongate the space and provide a visual link between the house and the garden.

For traditional conservatories, the colonial look works well with soft natural elements like rattan and wicker linking beautifully with the garden beyond. For a more modern approach, consider using modular corner seating and low-slung tables, keeping space and comfort to a maximum and clutter to a minimum. Give your new extension a sense of purpose, but remember to leave lots of circulation space. Occasional lighting is good and can be used in the evening to create a relaxed ambience.

Patios

A patio is no longer just a slab of uneven concrete in the backyard where the
dustbin lives. It has now come into its own, thanks to the popularity of timber
decking – the modern gardener's best friend. With varieties and designs to
suit all pockets, there's no excuse for not having something that looks neat
and well cared for. For low-cost decking the options are softwoods that have
been treated and grooved or planed. Timber like iroko or teak is outrageously
expensive and should only be chosen if the potential profit margin justifies
the outlay. Always check that your timber comes from sustainable forests, as
you don't want your patio literally to cost the earth, do you? As a general rule,
keep your patio design clean and simple and treat the space like an extra
room, creating a strong identity with furnishings, such as benches or a table
and chairs, and architectural plants in eye-catching containers.

Balconies

Balconies are the flat-dweller's patio and should be treated and decorated as
such. Most balconies come as an original feature, but don't despair if your
property doesn't have one because it may be possible to add one, planning
consent permitting. The great thing about balconies is that people tend to
think of them as exotic luxuries – maybe they remind us of our summer
holidays abroad – so they're a definite plus if you're selling.

An acquaintance of ours had a stunning apartment spread over the top two floors of a Georgian town-house in Edinburgh. Being Australian, he decided to create some outdoor space – somewhere to have his 'barbie'. He hooked up with a local architect and they drew up plans for an ornate steel balcony outside his kitchen/diner that was big enough to accommodate a portable barbecue and two seats. The original sash and casement window was converted into a split-level glass door. When he later put the flat up for sale he was inundated with offers. It was in the right location and, because of the balcony, it was more desirable than similar properties in the neighbourhood.

Gardens

A beautiful garden has the potential to be one of your home's most useful assets and we are all beginning to treat our outdoor space with as much care as the rooms inside our houses. Even if you hate gardening and can't afford to have your patch professionally landscaped, make sure it is tidy and attractive. If you have a young family, lawned areas for safe outdoor play will be important, but vast areas of blank green can be uninspiring for adults.

Unless you're an avid gardener, think of using hardy plants that require little care (your local garden centre will give you advice). Buy a few specimen plants and some sculptural shrubs to begin with. Try not to overplant though – keep everything simple and well spaced. A well-trimmed lawn always makes

Children's playhouses

Never underestimate the influence that children have when families are looking for a new home. Think back to the days when you were a child – don't you remember playing for hours in the garden with your friends and wishing you had a proper den, a place that was all your own? So if you live in a typical family home, why not create a special playhouse and see what effect it has on prospective buyers when their children discover it in the garden? It needn't be a huge building project requiring foundations or massive planning – an 'off-the-shelf' shed or small summerhouse anchored firmly on railway sleepers (buy them from your nearest reclamation yard) could be perfect. Another increasingly popular option is a tree house. These days there are specialist manufacturers (check the ads at the back of home interest magazines) who design and install off-the-ground bolt holes. The downside, of course, is building costs that you won't necessarily recoup when the time comes to sell. And don't forget to check your plans with your local planning authority.

a good impression, but if you don't have the time to look after it properly think about replacing it with paving, decking, natural stone chippings, decorative brickwork or a maintenance-free gravel garden. Make sure walls and fences are not falling down – if they are, not only will potential buyers think they will have to spend a lot of money replacing them, they may also fear that the property is vulnerable to intruders.

If the sale of your house is imminent there are several points to consider regarding your garden. Is there a shed to store tools for maintaining the lawn or flower beds? Is there more you can do to shield your garden from being overlooked? Maybe a few cleverly planted, fast-growing conifers could make all the difference (do avoid leylandii though). Or you could put up a fence with clever planting to stop it looking out of place – ask at your local garden centre for advice on plants that mature quickly. Is your garden an example of radical garden design? This could put buyers off and something that is seen as 'market unsuitable' could be a factor in diminishing your overall profits. See what you can do to tone it down.

A final point to consider is, to use one of our favourite terms, 'demographic specifics'. If your potential market is young urban professionals they may well have different expectations for their garden than other socio-economic groups. The thought of a large grassed area that needs time-consuming maintenance could be enough to send them scuttling elsewhere. Maybe a terraced area with pots and tubs would be a better use of the outdoor space. Speak to estate agents in your area to get their advice, and suss out the competition by keeping an eye on the local property press.

When we transformed properties for *The Million Pound Property Experiment* we always did as much as we could to create interesting and practical areas that would tempt buyers (see the individual case studies for details). However, this book was never destined to be a gardening bible, so our best basic advice is simply to apply the same planning principles to your garden as you would to the interior of your house, regardless of whether you're staying or selling on.

Front gardens

If you only have a small front garden it's still important to make the most of it. A well-stocked garden will give your house a sense of permanence and also enhance the property's pavement presence, making it much more marketable if you're selling on. Think about using a few hanging baskets on either side of the front door or a selection of colourful pots and tubs filled with a combination of evergreens and flowers.

Summerhouses and studios

A detached summerhouse or studio is an unattainable dream for most of us. For a start, you probably do need 'grounds' – the average suburban back garden is not going to be big enough for a proper summerhouse (as opposed to a potting shed) – and you will certainly need money.

A summerhouse or studio can be, planning permitting, whatever size you want it to be. Traditionally they are timber built, but there is nothing to stop your design being constructed from stone or brick – the choice is yours. When planning the positioning of windows take into account the way the sun moves round your garden – there is little point installing glazing where the sun doesn't reach. The summerhouse should also be designed so that air stays fresh and the inside temperature is controllable. A portable air-conditioning unit will be a godsend during particularly stuffy summers and heaters will allow the space to be used when the weather is less than perfect.

Outbuildings in a rear garden do not normally require planning permission if they are associated with the residential amenities of the house, and as long as they comply with certain regulations relating to position and size. However, it is always best to check beforehand whether you will need planning permission for any permanent structure, including walls, in a garden. Garages, sheds, greenhouses, summerhouses, gazebos and dog kennels are all classed as outbuildings, as are, believe it or not, swimming pools, aviaries and chicken runs. These are the main regulations governing outbuildings:

- The structure should not take up more than half of the available space.
- No part of the structure should extend beyond the original house limits on any side facing a public highway or footpath or service road.
- The height of the structure should not exceed 3 metres (10 feet), or 4 metres (13 feet) if it has a ridged roof.

Driveways

The approach to a property is the first thing visitors and buyers see, so it should always look as good as possible. The sound of 'crunchy' gravel is typically associated with wealth so, if you have enough space and if it will complement your property, consider investing in some. But don't make any major changes without first considering 'market specifics'. We made a mistake with our Harrogate property (see Case Study 4 on page 152), which was aimed at young families. Several potential buyers told us gravel was a definite minus. 'You try getting a pram across that!' was a common reaction.

House exterior

Whether you intend to move into your property for the short, medium or long term, it is absolutely crucial that you maintain its exterior to the best of your ability. If you let walls, windows or the roof go to rack and ruin there is every possibility that the interior may suffer as a direct consequence. At best, your home will deteriorate slowly over time; at worst, problems could compound very quickly and the situation become grave. Those slates blown off the roof during last winter's storms, for example, could have allowed water ingress that could subsequently dry out causing the onset of dry rot. What should have been a simple repair job if attended to straight away could escalate to a bill of thousands of pounds for eradication of the problem. The same applies to glazing. If pointing (the mastic or cement mix that holds window frames to exterior walls) starts to fall away and is not replaced immediately water could penetrate the walls, causing leaks and damage to the inside of your home. The message is clear – as soon as anything goes wrong with the exterior of the property, have it checked and repaired; not doing so will detract from the interior of your home, not to mention its future sale price and marketability.

▼ Make sure any additions, like conservatories or patios, are sympathetic to the existing house exterior.

Tyndalls Park Road, CLIFTON, BRISTOL

Property profile

A one-reception, two-bedroom flat with a skinny kitchen, a wedge-shaped bathroom, a boxroom and a big garden. Offers around £182,000. Freehold.

This was a home entirely down on its luck. Tenanted for many years, it was decoratively jaded with an overgrown garden at the rear, through which passage was necessary to get to the only door, which brought you into the kitchen. The poor configuration had put people off – that, together with the overgrown approach to the front of the building and the fact that there was no allocated parking.

Our first offer of £165,000 was initially accepted, but unexpectedly turned down later. Still confident of ample profit we reoffered £179,000 – the lowest price the agent said his client would consider. Two days later an agreement was reached and several weeks on we took possession. Here are our sums:

Buying price:	£179,000
Buying costs:	£2000
Development costs:	£44,000
Selling costs:	£4000
Selling price:	£231,000
Profit:	£2000

At the heart of Bristol's new media district, this potentially impressive two-bedroom garden apartment – little more than a dingy basement flat accessed from the rear when we stumbled across it – was in need of urgent rebranding. We needed to reinvent it, creating a fashionable interior that utilized the available space to the optimum, perfect for both single buyers and young professional couples.

Location

Bristol, as the largest city in the south-west of England and with a population of approximately half a million, is a wonderful destination. A few miles from its centre two motorways intersect – the M4 from London to south Wales bridges the Severn before the river widens to become the Bristol Channel and the north–south M5 skirts the city at Avonmouth. Add to that substantial rail and international air and sea links and you'll understand that Bristol is well connected for transportation to the Midlands, Wales and London. Consequently, these factors have gone at least some of the way towards helping Bristol to rebrand and become a 'hot spot' with its burgeoning industry, tourist appeal and booming local economy.

Why Clifton?

Ask anyone in the property 'know' about where best to buy in Bristol and they'll almost definitely tell you to head for the affluent and bustling area known as Clifton. The housing stock in this leafy district comprises characterful Georgian town houses (many of which have been subdivided into smaller privately owned homes), apartments, offices and rented accommodation, all serviced by a plethora of coffee shops, furniture stores, bars and cafés.

Our plans

This particular property, while hugely exciting, presented a catalogue of difficult problems. But hey, if you want to make serious money you've got to be ready to face all manner of challenges. Poor 'room flow', tired run-down décor, horrible dark kitchen, rear entrance problems, unruly garden, problematic parking and a general lack of identity made this the kind of overlooked property for which we're always on the lookout.

We wanted to create a precise and considered space that would appeal to Bristol's burgeoning workforce, many of whom are employed in television, education, communications or 'new technology'. We assembled a 'focus group' and, over a 'power' breakfast, asked them what they look for in an ideal home. Their answers were clear and unanimous – at least two bedrooms, a second WC, a sleek contemporary tiled bathroom, a separate state-of-the-art wet room/shower and ultramodern kitchen design employing lots of timber and steel. Ideally, they all wanted a garden but because of professional time constraints it would have to be low maintenance. A decked area would be a bonus and, as for the internal colour scheme, well, everything should be neutral and low-key.

To fulfil these wishes, we decided to open up the internal partitioned hallway to house a funky kitchen/dining room, while ripping out the existing kitchen and replacing it with a pared down second bedroom. A small 'change of address' was also on the cards as we planned to

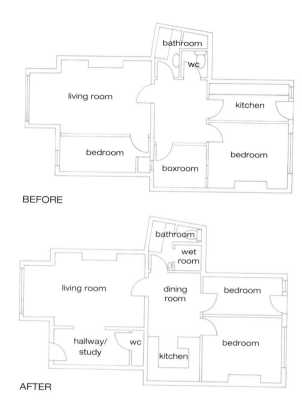

▲ Even with its poor configuration, we could see that a change of orientation could point this apartment in the right direction.

relocate the front door from the rear of the house to the front, thus allowing us to create a patio approach as a grand entrance to the apartment. A slick bathroom and integral wet room could be formed, and a second loo created in an area of a new hallway/study where the second bedroom had previously been located. All change!

So, there would be the major building work needed to convert the space, some minor rising-damp treatment, the replastering of all the rooms and the ripping out and repositioning of the kitchen, as well as normal additions like central heating, rewiring and replumbing – all before we could start colouring and dressing the property as an executive apartment.

Moving the front door

Our first alteration meant creating a doorway at the front of the building where there was a window to the small front bedroom. We took a real gamble and decided to start this alteration before getting planning permission – our project manager was already in discussion with the local planning department and, from his initial conversations with them, he could see no reason why permission would be refused. Our advice to you, however, is not to do this! We didn't have the luxury of time on our hands and had to take a calculated risk. Fortunately it paid off, but had the decision gone the other way we might have had to close up the new doorway and rebuild the window.

▶ A new 'portholed' door provides a modern design element to bring this space bang up to date.

The hallway/study space

To change the position of the front door, the front bedroom became the hallway. We closed up the original door to the bedroom and opened up an archway into the living room to create a semi-open-plan configuration. One wall was lined with mirrors to increase the feeling of space and light, and the room was painted in a neutral shade. Colour and identity were added through artwork and via the inclusion of a modern table and chair, which encouraged potential buyers to see it as an identifiable room and not just a corridor (see page 102). Seamless laminate flooring started here and was laid throughout most of the house to provide unity between rooms.

The living room

The main change was in orientation, with access moving from a door at the edge of the wall to the off-centre archway between the living room and the hallway/study space. The entire room was replastered and tiny modern spotlights were studded across the ceiling. A non-functioning fireplace was opened up and a modern wooden shelf added underneath to give the room a focal point (see page 120). Lining the aperture with inexpensive slate tiles helped to provide a sharp modern touch. Further style direction was added through artwork and contemporary furnishings that were in keeping with the clean square lines of the whole apartment. The door leading through to the kitchen/dining room was 'portholed' to add another simple design feature.

The kitchen/dining room

This was previously an awkward space, split in two by a wobbly partition wall, to provide a boxroom and an inner hallway. Both without windows, these spaces were virtually useless and had put potential buyers off. We decided to knock down the wall and build a stunning kitchen and dining room in this space.

Although we gave the room two functions, it was important to consider it as one in terms of design, so we employed a colour scheme that would suit both. We chose a modern oak kitchen from Ikea, with outsized handles for extra modernity (see page 79). Applying a similar wood veneer on the far wall of the dining space, and using a matching larder unit as a dining-room dresser, tied the two areas together perfectly. The veneer wall was added not only to provide a designer touch but also to hide the fact that the bathroom was in the next room (see page 91).

▲ The ultimate bathroom indulgence – a walk-in wet room.

Equipping this room probably looks like it cost the earth, but in actual fact it didn't break the bank. By shopping wisely from catalogue-return shops and scratch-and-dent stores we were able to buy an integrated washer-dryer, a steel-style fridge-freezer and a stainless-steel range for the cost of standard options. Remember – it's not how much you spend that matters, it's how you spend it!

The bathroom

This room was potentially difficult to redesign because of its strange shape, but it actually worked well in the end. First, we knocked out the wall that separated it from the existing toilet and in doing so created sufficient space for a walk-in wet room/shower. Next, we repositioned the toilet in a 'niche' in the corner of the bathroom to keep it well and truly hidden away. We opted for a white bathroom suite and, to simplify further, tiled the whole space wall-to-wall in warm natural shades. Indulging the 'look' with special taps, and extras like a fab white bowl-sink, made a huge difference even when they were teamed with a standard bath and toilet. Modern wall lights completed the look and the finished product was everything a bathroom should be – practical and extremely beautiful (see pages 83 and 121).

The separate toilet

A cupboard-like walkway between the living room and the new hallway was closed up and converted into a separate toilet. That way guests could use washroom facilities without having to go into the owner's personal bathroom. Again, we kept the look clean and neutral.

Bedroom one

Luckily the master bedroom was huge, so we designed it to have the same degree of impact as the living room with clean lines, ample space

▼ Here a fireplace and coordinating artwork provide a strong focal point for the master bedroom.

and simple styling. The room was completely replastered and a fireplace feature was carved out of one wall to provide a modern focal point like the one in the living room (see below). With an eye on our budget we created our own artworks by masking off stripes of grey on the inside of inexpensive frames, which tied in perfectly with the grey bouclé curtains. Comfort, as usual, was an important consideration so we opted for a plain but indulgent wool carpet.

Bedroom two

This room had been the kitchen – and an ugly, dark blue, woodchip-walled one to boot! We stripped the space completely bare of all wall coverings, kitchen units, tiles and pipe work before a clever little cupboard was created to house the new central heating boiler. Next, the whole room was replastered to provide smooth flat walls. Plastering, as far as we are concerned, makes a huge difference to any room and the whole procedure, while laborious, is well worth spending money on. We kept the door to the garden where it was and dressed the space with a daybed to accommodate guests or as an additional sitting room (see page 141). The room's lack of width was a real problem, but with no scope to extend (and with no more money to spend!) we simply put up … and shut up.

Outside

In this area of Bristol car parking is a major concern. To solve this we approached the other owners in the building and simply asked them to help us clean out the front garden, cut back the lawned area and create dedicated, gravelled parking that could accommodate all who lived there. It cost a couple of hundred pounds for

the gravel, but we were prepared to invest in the outside to make selling the inside easier.

Next, the well at the front of the property was covered with decking and, with this done, the whole area was painted white. We added spun aluminium planters laden with box-hedge to bring life to the space and, finally, a stylish table and bench set to suggest real function (see above). When you're selling it's important not to overlook the value of any space, so treat it all with equal priority and don't leave it up to potential buyers to work out how they'd use it.

Estate agency time

With work complete, we invited several local agents to put a price on our apartment. Each one waxed lyrical about the splendour of the interior and assured us that securing a buyer would be an easy task. With quoted values around the £255,000 mark, we became rather excited.

We picked a company who appeared to be catering for the market we were trying to attract. They quickly secured us an offer of £250,000, but this collapsed just before contracts were due to exchange, and we didn't seem able to find

▲ To entice buyers in, we made the approach to the property beautiful as well as practical.

another buyer. This may have been due, in part, to the fact that we were selling in summer. Getting jumpy, as weeks turned into months, we tried another local agent in a desperate attempt to move on. We couldn't understand what the problem was – everyone liked the apartment but nobody seemed to want to commit. Potential buyers highlighted the size of the second bedroom and the fact that the only access to the garden was through this room. Other than these points, however, there was little to suggest the apartment had any selling 'issues', but the sale was taking much longer than we had imagined.

Eventually we instructed a third agent and a lower price of £239,950 was agreed. We accepted an offer of £237,500, but this was then withdrawn due to the buyer's ill health. Eventually, nine months later, we accepted an offer of £231,000 and completed successfully. By then, however, our profit had declined and was now rather disappointing. It had been a long and arduous path, which had put a strain on our hard-working team and on us, but at least we were on the move.

As soon as you've made the decision to sell the time has come to be resolute and ruthless. If you follow the simple guidelines set out in this section you'll discover that the whole selling process can be made much easier and certainly far less daunting than you expect. At the end of the day you survived the experience of buying your home. Selling, by comparison, should be a doddle – just as long as you remain fully informed and on the ball at every turn.

LING

The right time to sell

When marketing any product timing is extremely important if you want to maximize your profit – after all, there would be no point trying to sell Christmas cards at Easter. What this boils down to is: put your property on the market when it's looking its best. For example, if you've got a fantastic garden sell the house, if you can afford to wait, at the beginning of summer when everything is in full bloom.

However, we can't always determine for ourselves when we might have to move house so it's crucial to find ways of extending the marketability of a property throughout the year. Of course, if you own a great house in a popular area you should have no problem selling whenever you wish, but if you want to maximize your profits, or if you live in a not so popular area, try to think of ways of showing off the best features of your home. For example, if you do have a wonderfully colourful garden take pictures of it when it's at its most attractive to illustrate how lovely it can be. Or take pictures of rooms that fill up with sunlight on bright sunny days. This will prove invaluable if you're selling in the winter months. Remember – selling your home requires

▼ Plan in advance – if you anticipate selling your property in the dark winter months, take some photos in the summer so you can allow viewers a glimpse of your home at its very best.

major merchandising. After all, you're not just selling bricks and mortar, you're selling a dream and getting the timing right is all part of that.

If there are any really negative points to the property try to limit those that may put buyers off. If your house is dark, for example, market it when the days are dullest – that way potential buyers will blame the weather for the lack of illumination, and you can set an attractive mood with lighting. Of course, if you do decide to follow the advice in this book to the letter you're sure to keep moving upmarket whatever the time of year.

When to sell

When it comes to selling property spring is traditionally the best time of year. Christmas is long past and the short dark days of winter are giving way to longer sunny days announcing the start of summer. At this time people tend to think of two things: moving house, particularly in time to relax over the summer; and planning holidays. Both are areas that involve spending money.

Autumn is another time when things are buoyant. Summer holidays are becoming just a distant memory in September and October and the property market once again springs into life. With people planning for the year ahead, spurred on by children starting a new term at school and the desire to move to a new home in time for Christmas, estate agency offices are bursting with ripe new properties and scores of buyers ready to harvest the cream of the crop.

Consequently, with the market awash with people looking for property and with properties for sale, competition can be steep. This makes your approach to selling and presenting your home even more important.

When not to sell

The high summer months and the Christmas festive period are the worst times to try and sell a property as people have other things to spend their money on and keep them busy – namely, overseas holidays and the expense of Christmas and New Year celebrations. Of course, there will always be someone looking for property, but at this time of year estate agents' windows are more likely to be filled with old 'sold' rather than new 'for sale' signs.

On the plus side, when the pickings are lean local estate agents are likely to offer a more personal service, given that they don't have so many clients to deal with. This means you can keep in in regular contact with your agent and can build up a friendly working relationship with him or her. This approach costs nothing but brings rich rewards and, of course, makes the whole selling process a much happier and less stressful prospect.

▲ Sell your home whatever the weather – fresh flowers bring a summery feel all year round, whilst cosy mood lighting will add warmth to a room.

Methods of selling

Having made your home as marketable as you can, it's time to face the next stage of the profitability process. It's time to let your audience know you're out there – time to sell, sell, sell. It's all very well having a wonderful product but if nobody knows about it all your efforts will be wasted.

Many of the points we would normally raise on this subject are similar to those we've already covered in Property sources (see page 26), but there are several other ways to promote the optimum selling environment and find your prime buyer … So hang on in there.

Surveys

If you're selling a property the onus is on the buyer to instruct a surveyor to determine the value of your home. However, if you have concerns about your property's worth or if you simply want to get an accurate valuation – independently of your estate agent – a survey report is critical.

▲ The first person you'll have to impress is your estate agent, so make sure every room delivers the 'wow' factor when they come round.

Selling alone

The best way to sell a home will vary from property to property. If, traditionally, houses in your street are snapped up it might be worth considering a private sale if you feel confident you can cope without the help of an agent. You could save yourself a fortune if you go it alone. It is a good idea to speak to local estate agents in the first instance, though, to establish the marketability and the true value of your home. Invite two or three round (most offer a free, no-obligation valuation service) and ask them about the prices traditionally achieved for your type of property. The next stage is to choose a lawyer to take care of conveyancing and to advise you. Basically, the more information you have the better.

After this, there is absolutely nothing to stop you putting together your own individual property package. Leafleting need not be expensive and printers can put together a flier for less than £100. Either deliver these at random in your specified area or persuade a local newsagent to insert them into the newspapers he delivers. While you may wonder whether all this effort is worth it, all it takes is the interest of one person to effect a mutually suitable sale and purchase. Who knows – maybe the prospective buyer of your home has a real aversion to estate agents and would be glad of the opportunity to give them a wide berth.

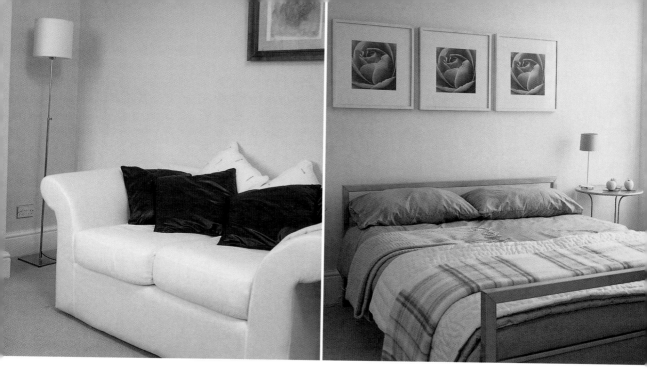

Estate agents

Estate agents have a poorer reputation than they deserve, due to a few devious sharks who have tarnished the image of their profession. However, they are one of the most obvious avenues to follow when you want to climb the property ladder and, as such, they attract volume interest from potential buyers.

Look carefully at the heading above. What does it say? That's right, it says 'estate agents' – agents (persons acting on your behalf) for your estate (property). They are working for you, so make sure you get your money's worth. Communication is the vital word here, so it's absolutely crucial that you develop a good relationship with your agent. Ask questions and demand progress reports – call them every day for an update. Ask for regular feedback from prospective buyers on every aspect of the sale – positive or otherwise. Demand an honest opinion of the saleability of your property so that you can tweak it accordingly. Remember – you are paying for their service and are entitled to good value for your money. A good agent will work hard for your sale. And a major plus is that they will arrange all the viewings, something which you might find difficult to organize efficiently if you are selling on your own.

Don't opt for just one valuation. Instead, invite several agents who specialize in your area to give you their opinions. Previous selling history is not, however, always a true indication of what you can expect to achieve. Use past pricing as a general guide only, and remember that if your property is below standard in any way the chances are that a lower price would be more realistic. However, the opposite also applies – if you're selling a fully restored house in a popular street you should expect to achieve a higher price.

There's no point having agents around if you're not going to ask the right questions, so consider the following points:

- Are they the right agents for the job? Look at their current property portfolio. Does it include similar properties to your own? Are they specialists in your immediate geographical area, and are they going to expose your property to the most relevant market? Don't just sit there guessing, ask them!

- How do they present themselves as a company? Look at their office, their stationery, the quality of their home-brochure photography and their adverts in the property pages – do they appeal to you? If not, the chances are they won't appeal to potential buyers.

- Ask about turnover – how quickly do properties of a similar type sell in the area? Ask about past performance – how much did they achieve for a similar property three streets away?

Which agent?

There are many different selling packages. Some agents may offer 'free' advertising, others may offer 'free' set-up costs. Remember, however, that there is generally no such thing as a free lunch and, accordingly, if an agent appears to be making indulgent promises of a 'free this' and a 'free that' there is probably a hidden cost somewhere else or an inflated commission. Find out exactly what is included in the price they quote – ask about sales brochures, house photos, website advertising and floor plans. It could be that their glossy brochure is reserved solely for properties over a certain price or that there's a surcharge for appearing in it, so ask first before committing yourself to anything.

From our own experiences, selling privately and for *The Million Pound Property Experiment*, we have discovered that it's not necessarily the agent who suggests the highest price who will offer you the best chance of a successful sale. Most will have your best interests at heart, but some may be a little 'adventurous' in their valuations. Listen to and digest all of the available information (it will do you no end of good to be up to speed on *every* issue) and make an informed decision on who should sell your home. Be positive, however, as there are many well-intentioned and experienced agents who will serve you well. We have happily sold many properties through standard estate agencies without encountering any problems whatsoever. Work with your agent and you will find the experience a rewarding one.

Beating estate agents at their own game

There should exist true trust between you and your agent. After all, you've chosen them and you are paying a lot of money for their services, but you should be watchful nevertheless. If you suspect that things are not going according to your original plan, get a friend to phone up and ask for details of your property to be sent to them. Get someone else to ring up to enquire about viewing. If everything seems to be OK, fine, but if your friends suspect you're not getting the service you deserve confront your agent immediately. Ask for a weekly report and insist on feedback after every viewing – hopefully your confidence and assertiveness will inspire them. Ask for your property details to be sent out along with similar properties they are handling. This is a simple blag to save on advertising costs, but one that could really make a difference.

Negotiating commission

If you decide to appoint one agent this is known as a sole agency agreement. Commission rates vary, but most agents will charge between 1.5% and 2.5% of the selling price for sole agency rights. If you appoint several agents, to try to expose the property to more people, this is known as a multi-agency agreement and the fee charged will normally be slightly higher. Sometimes two agents will work together to sell one property, which is referred to as a joint sole agency agreement; again the commission will be higher than with a sole agency agreement. (Personally, we think it's best to try one agency first, as there's nothing that smacks of desperation more than several different sales boards littering your front garden – a potential buyer will assume you're in need of a quick sale and will be more likely to submit a lower offer.)

If you know things are currently sluggish in your area it is definitely worth haggling over the final percentage. If you can knock 2.5% down to 1.5% you'll save a fortune. We prefer to arrange a tailored and individual selling package. The 'sliding scale', our favourite, is a great way forward. Basically, the higher the figure your agent achieves, the more you pay them. Let's say you have a home worth £100,000 that you want to sell and your agent is earning 2% of the sale price. Whether they get you a price of £95,000 or £100,000, they still earn the same 2% – i.e. £1900 for £95,000 or £2000 for £100,000. If they're scared to push higher than £95,000 for fear of losing the sale, all they stand to lose in shortfall terms is £100. They've got a sale, or as near as dammit, and they aren't likely to jeopardize it for the sake of £100, are they? But you, the seller? Well, you're down £5000. In a situation such as this, negotiate. Why not promise, for example, another £200 for every extra £1000 they can bring in on top of the original offer? You're still getting the remaining £800 in every £1000 so the scales are balanced heavily in your favour. Clever, huh?

Alternative sales strategies

Our favourite strategy to date is one we used for the Bristol flat in *The Million Pound Property Experiment* (see Case Study 3 on page 118). When we had finished working on the property we decided to work with our estate agent to create a rather different selling plan than normal. Anticipating that our target buyers would be from the cool new media market (Bristol is awash with TV, radio and computer-related industries) we decided to try a new marketing strategy – a drinks reception in the house with enough oriental finger-food to keep the conveyor belts at Yo Sushi rolling for ever. On this occasion, more than ever before, it was all about setting the scene. We splashed out on good wines and a million canapés to suggest an extravagant lifestyle. We put Kruder Dorfmeister on low and dressed to impress. The night was more like an exclusive première to which only those in the know had been invited. It gave us an opportunity to answer every question each interested guest threw at us – 'How has this job been done?', 'What material was used for that job?', 'Is this a new boiler, and is it still under guarantee?', 'Why have you chosen wood veneer walls? Are they still going to be cool in two years' time?' and so on. It was the perfect opportunity to make big statements about what we were selling and we loved it. The evening was a resounding success. One or two people expressed an initial interest, which immediately got the ball rolling. It's the old story – the more one person wants something, the more appealing it becomes to others. News of the property spread by word of mouth and buyers started to call our agent before he contacted them. Now that's what we call success!

Virtual marketing

There are an increasing number of websites dedicated to property selling so use a search engine to track down one that suits your needs. Many local estate agents have agreements with umbrella internet sites that feature properties across the country. Sites like www.assertahome.com, www.findaproperty.co.uk and www.fish4homes.co.uk all offer a national network of properties, as well as advice on buying and selling. This method of selling is a good way of exposing your property to a larger market, outside your local area, and is best used in conjunction with a local estate agent to cover the home market as well.

Newspaper features

This is one of our favourite avenues but it only works when you have a particularly strong product to sell. If there is something unique about your property it might be worth getting in touch with your local newspaper and asking them if they want to do an editorial feature on it. Is it a converted shop? Has it got the most amazing roof-space carved out of a previously redundant office building? You get the gist … Develop your networking skills and see if you can find someone who knows the local journalists so that you personally can interest them in your story. We were lucky enough to find a local newspaper to run a piece on our Bristol property. The amazing, attention-grabbing story, which highlighted our 'state of the art kitchen', 'precision bathroom and wet room' and 'huge private gardens', really registered with potential buyers and we were overrun with interest. We knew we had created something pretty special but the response was actually quite humbling.

Full-on public announcement

Again, on a product-specific basis, there are various things you can do that will excite huge interest. And you don't need to go so far as to organize a champagne reception for your potential buyers. In Glasgow, our home town, a developer we know hired a publicity truck to drive around the West End for a weekend to promote an apartment he'd just developed. He put a picture of the property on each side of the van, made sure people knew how to contact him and then sat back and waited for the phone to ring. He had more than 30 enquiries and he sold the apartment within two weeks with a closing date that attracted five offers.

Auction

Selling by auction is not generally seen as a first port of call as auctions tend to feature properties that are difficult to sell or those that have been 'stuck' for some time. Buyers, traditionally, are always looking for a bargain at an auction, and you'd have to be really lucky to sell for a decent price. On the plus side, prospective auction buyers have to prove to auctioneers that they are in a position to buy immediately, so there's less chance of becoming involved in a chain where you'll have to wait for your buyer to sell before you can progress up the property ladder. If you do choose to sell by auction, set yourself a price range and stick to it. The auctioneer can withdraw your property from the auction sale if the desired price is not achieved.

Preparing to sell

Before you put your property on the market take a good look at it. If there is anything that needs repairing fix it, and if there is anything that looks worn replace it. If you don't want to splash out on a new sofa or chairs, spruce up the old ones with fabulous throws or a selection of snuggly cushions. Put yourself in a viewer's position and do a few sums as you walk around. How much would it cost to replace the carpets, for example, or to install a new bathroom suite or redecorate the master bedroom? It may seem like an unnecessary expense, but if you are prepared to spend a few hundred pounds on brightening the property up you could stop a buyer trying to shave a few thousand pounds off the asking price because the place looks so shabby.

One thing that costs next to nothing, except a bit of elbow grease, is cleaning, so get out the bleach and tackle the mildew on the tile grout and the dust on the skirting boards. Clean and polish all windows and mirrors until they are spotless: you'll be amazed at how much brighter everything looks.

▲ LEFT: You only get one chance to make a first impression. Get your buyers 'sold' before they've even stepped through the front door.
RIGHT: And if you haven't got a topiary-lined front garden, then a freshly painted front door and gleaming windows are a great introduction to what lies beyond.

Lighting

- The best light to promote is that which Mother Nature offers in abundance – daylight. Allow it to flood into your home by pulling back curtains and opening blinds. Replace standard bulbs with blue 'natural' daylight ones.
- Artificial lighting can help minimize problems. Try mood lighting to make a dull sitting room look cosy, and bright lighting to illuminate kitchens and rooms that get little natural light.
- Outdoor lighting will ensure the garden can be seen in the evenings, as well as lifting the appearance of your home if it's located in a dark and dingy area.
- If your home is of architectural significance consider illuminating the exterior with ground lights set on an angle, to show off its beauty by night and make it irresistible to buyers.

On-street presence

When improving your home to capture the optimum market it's all too easy to overlook the bit that buyers see first – the exterior. Whether you're selling a compact terraced house with nothing more than a small step between it and the rest of the world or a large detached home with generous gardens and driveway, it's vital to make sure all exterior aspects look perfect.

Put yourself in a viewer's position. What do you see as you approach your front door? A vision of exterior perfection or a hotchpotch of unfinished jobs? Poor paintwork, crumbling masonry and an overgrown garden? While your home may be a testament to design within, if it looks disappointing from the outside viewers will have made up their minds before they have even crossed the threshold. The best remedy is to do as much as you possibly can. Some work done is better than none at all, so get busy before your estate agent takes the photographs and your potential buyers arrive. Make good anything that looks unloved and your chances of a successful sale will increase tenfold. What might seem like an enormous problem or chore to potential buyers may, in actual fact, be a small task that you could put right over a weekend.

Windows are as good a place to start as any. Even the uninitiated home buyer will pay particular attention to this area and there is, in our experience, something ritualistic about scanning and prodding glass and timber. Just as naive car buyers walk around vehicles and make snap decisions by kicking the tyres, so too will viewers estimate the general worth of a property by checking the state of the glazing. But don't overspend. An entire window replacement scheme might make your home more attractive, but if the cost won't be reflected in your sale price don't do it. There are, for example, specialist companies who will work around what you already have to improve the situation. Rotted sills or astragals can be replaced, while draughtproofing can be improved with the addition of side 'brushes' or inexpensive foam sections.

Repainting the windows might be all that you need to do to improve the general appearance of the exterior of your property and make it a much more attractive prospect. Simple procedures like these can help to reduce not only noise and draughts but also your viewers' worries about repairs that appear to be more troublesome than they actually are.

If your home doesn't look loved on the outside the chances are it's not loved on the inside. Viewers make their minds up about a property within the first few minutes of seeing it, so make sure it's a positive impression that they get from the moment they first set eyes on your home – and get that sale in the bag.

Red flags

No one knows your home better than you do and, consequently, no one knows its little foibles like you do. You know the sort of thing – squeaky floorboards, loose tiles, cracked windowpanes. But don't just sit back and expect viewers not to notice – do something about it. Imperfections, however small they seem, become 'red flags' to viewers and 'red flags' spell danger. There are no such things as problems, only solutions, so think carefully and try to eradicate any areas of negativity. Before you start the viewing process ask a friend or your estate agent to walk round the property and point out any 'red flags' you may have missed because you see them every day.

▶ Just like framing a picture, stylish gates opening on to a front driveway add to a property's appeal and allude to a grand lifestyle.

Ten ways to improve your on-street presence

1 Make sure the name or number of the house is clearly visible and that the street sign is apparent. You do, after all, want potential buyers to find your property, don't you?

2 Make sure your front garden is tidy with pathways clearly defined. Trim hedges, mow lawns, prune back unruly bushes and weed, weed, weed. If space allows, give your garden a purpose – if it's decorative fill it with beautiful flowers; if it's a suntrap pop a bench in.

3 Lose the trash – if your dustbins are at the front of the house hide them away in timber-built housing or put a fence around them in an out-of-the-way area at the side of the garden. Whatever you do, just keep them hidden!

4 Extend a warm welcome by repainting your front door. We think deep blue or deep red are the best colours as they suggest elegance and style. You could just clean or replace the existing door furniture and add a welcome mat.

5 Establish your boundaries with fencing between you and your neighbours' properties so that potential buyers know exactly what they're getting. If your fence is past its 'use by' date, replace it and make sure your front gate is swinging properly and not propped up waiting to fall off.

6 Balance the exterior of your house by making sure all curtains and blinds are hung properly.

7 Hanging baskets, window boxes and planters are a great way of adding a splash of natural colour, but make sure you water them every day – you don't want any dead plants hanging around.

8 If your front garden is boring add a statue or a water feature, something that will give your space personality and help it stick in a buyer's mind.

9 Maintain your property – make sure there are no obviously unattended problems. Check the pointing, clear and mend the guttering, and free the downpipes of rust. Clean up brickwork and repaint grubby rendering.

10 Make sure your house is adequately lit, and that the lighting makes the house look as good by night as it does by day.

Staging

This may sound rather strange but selling your home should be approached in exactly the same way as putting on a stage play. Both call for stunning sets and great performances and both must satisfy the paying public if they are to be successful. Sure, you might just want to sell and move on, but if you're aiming to maximize the financial return careful merchandising and attention to detail are paramount. After all, you're not just selling your home, you are sharing and furthering a dream.

First impressions count

We are by now all familiar with the phrase 'first impressions count' and in the home-selling situation this is critical. It's like going on a first date: even if you're not into dressing to impress, you still make an effort. At the very least you will clean your teeth and have a shave. Heck, you might even squirt on a little aftershave. And the girls? Well, you'll root through your make-up bag for your favourite lipstick and go all out to knock 'em dead. A new suit? Well, why not? A visit to the hairdresser? Well, it might just make that person on the other side of your *pasta con quattro formaggi* like you a little bit more. Yup, you're learning: it's that first impression thing again. Of course, your date will eventually like you for your personality but for now, whether you like it or not, they're marking you out of 10 on what they see first. And it's exactly the same thing with your property.

> ### Furniture sources
>
> If resources are limited when it comes to dressing your property, think about borrowing furniture from friends and family. Don't mismatch though – try to create a cohesive identity for each room. Second-hand and charity shops, catalogue-return stores and discount retail outfits are also good sources. If you're still stuck for household effects think about employing the services of a furniture rental company. This new venture is slowly gathering momentum here after years of success in the United States. The rental company will have a vast warehouse of items on display – you decide on what you want, and for how long, before agreeing on a price. Ensure the company's stock is covered either by their insurance or your own and, as you would in a normal purchase situation, measure each item first to ensure it fits in your home.

▲ Dress to impress – use colourful accessories to set the tone of a room and attract potential buyers.

Setting the scene inside

Walk into Selfridges or Harvey Nichols and look around – do you see piles of clothes and shoes scattered everywhere? No, of course you don't, so why go for this look when it comes to selling your home? Do not underestimate the power of the 'wow' factor: stunning homes make for stunning profits. Merchandising is just as important at home as it is in a department store, so here are a few points to help you present your home with pride.

▼ Remember, you're selling yourself and your lifestyle as well as your home. Merchandise carefully and make sure all your most stylish items are on display.

- You've heard it a million times, but here it is again – clutter puts people off and does nothing to help sell houses. *You* might not have noticed the gradual build-up of family knick-knacks and life's general debris but your viewers certainly will. To you, each trinket is a familiar object but to them each one is just another symptom of a messy room and lifestyle. Some viewers won't have the vision to see past your clutter, so do them a favour and have a major spring clean, whatever time of year you choose to sell. Then you'll free up the most valuable commodity of any home – *space*!

- Remember that viewers will want to open your cupboards and drawers and check how deep the shelves are, so make sure they are not filled to overflowing. Overstacked shelves, whether laden with new media paraphernalia, books or CDs, will show that there simply isn't enough space for an ordered life. So have a good clear-out and free up as much storage space as you can.

- Remove any overpowering elements of your personality. Prospective buyers will generally want to imagine *their* lives taking place in *your* space. We are not suggesting drastic home surgery, merely some gentle pinning and tucking. Take your family photographs off the walls and replace them with framed prints that work with your décor. If you can't bear to remove every portrait leave just one group snapshot on the mantelpiece.

- One of the most important aspects of home-selling is cleanliness. Whether you like it or not, viewers will judge you and your space by the standard of hygiene on display. You wouldn't buy a car if the ashtrays were full and if the windows were dirty, so why should you expect someone to buy a house in a similarly unsavoury state? Kitchens and bathrooms in particular should be shown in sparkling showroom condition, as these are both rooms that are sold 'fully furnished'. If, however, you just can't find time to haul out the Hoover call for the assistance of your nearest Molly Maids.

- Empty rooms *don't* sell houses – while it might seem like a good idea to leave rooms unfurnished to show the space, this can be off-putting as viewers often fail to see the potential of vacant space. Don't overstamp your individual personality on a room but do try and spell out, using a few tasteful furnishings, its potential.

Be honest

Answer *everything* honestly. If potential buyers ask questions and discover elsewhere that you have been economical with the truth they'll doubt every piece of information you've given them.

Finishing touches

Your living space may have only a few pieces of furniture but if they're not properly placed you'll give the impression of a cramped environment. Arrange sofas, chairs and tables in such a way as to allow viewers to walk around freely. There's little point in having a wonderful view if a massive table or sofa stops a potential buyer walking over to the window to enjoy it. If, after all this, your furniture still dominates consider more drastic action. Take a tip from new-home builders and use smaller pieces to create the illusion of space. If necessary, put your existing furniture into storage and invest in several more compact pieces. Don't worry too much about the cost – sensible buying at this stage will mean you can reuse your 'investment' furniture in your new home. Simply plan ahead. If your second bedroom is large enough to take a double bed make sure it has one; don't just shove in a single bed and leave your viewers wondering if the room is large enough. Remember, a double bed says double room. It's as simple as that. But don't squash a double bed into a room that barely has space for it. Put in a single bed instead, and perhaps an armchair or desk to show that the room could double as a study or office.

In all the bedrooms create a tasteful, neutral colour scheme that allows for seasonal adjustment – piles of chunky throws and extra blankets for winter and oceans of soft dreamy fabrics for summer should ensure your room will appeal to viewers whatever the time of year. Fabric and lots of it is an easy way to add opulence to a bedroom. Billowing curtains suggest luxury, romance and comfort – key elements in any bedroom! Crisp white cotton linens are an everyday luxury that no one should be without. It's even worth sending your bedlinen to the local laundry to be washed and pressed for hotel-standard comfort and freshness. There's nothing to beat that 'just ironed' look when your viewers arrive!

When it comes to selecting the household objects you should have on display, think style icons – Alessi juicers, balsamic vinegar and Dualit toasters say quality kitchen more than cans of supermarket own-brand baked beans and tubs of margarine. You need to suggest to viewers the lifestyle that will be available to them when they buy your home. In the bathroom, keep smells sweet and sexy and avoid drawing attention to its 'toileting' aspect. Keep spare toilet rolls and other items of personal hygiene stored discreetly away and lock pills and potions in a cabinet. Make sure your toilet seat has a lid.

Plants and fresh flowers are a great way of filling space and adding life and colour to a room, but make sure they are healthy and tidy. There's

▲ Impeccably dressed rooms with the comfort factor may be enough to tempt potential buyers to sign on the dotted line.

nothing more off-putting than dead plants consuming room space. Flowers should be fresh, clean and in plenty of water. And remember, viewers are examining you as much as they are your home, so do try to look your best. Maybe it's not *just* your house they're after, but also your lifestyle!

Pets

As devoted animal-lovers and keepers of two fine felines, namely Winston and Felix, it pains us to say that pets really don't win prizes when it comes to selling your home. As many as three out of five households may indeed have a dog or a cat, but if your hot buyer is one of the uninitiated your furry friends might just be enough to send him or her scuttling off elsewhere. So keep pets in the garden, pop them over to your neighbour for the afternoon or get a friend to take them for a walk – just make sure they're not curled up on your sofa when your viewers arrive.

The viewing

When the time comes to sell one of the most important people in your life will be your estate agent. Imagine you are entertaining a theatre critic and give them, and every potential buyer, an Oscar-winning performance.

Try and tailor the environment to appeal to each viewing as far as you can. Selling a house is like selling anything – you've got to know your product and you've got to know your market. Ask your agent for some details about who is viewing. Do they have a family? Are they single? Male or female? Then adjust your sales approach accordingly. Would a car salesman push the speedier aspects of a new car over safety if he were selling to a family? Similarly, if a family is viewing, tell them about the positive family-orientated aspects of the property, such as its child-safe garden, its quiet street and the fact that other families live nearby. Don't expect viewers to know it all because they won't. State the obvious and sell, sell, sell.

Use your senses

Take a multisensory approach to showing your home – not only do the visuals have to be right; think about sounds, smells, taste and touch. Your home should comfort and cosset potential buyers, so think of making them a great cup of coffee while soothing their souls with some ambient music. Nobody wants to hear a juggernaut crash by as they wander through your space, so keep your windows firmly closed while viewings take place if you live close to a busy main road. Conversely, if outside noises such as birdsong or waterfalls are your backdrop throw open your windows and welcome them in. Offer viewers olfactory titillation through scented candles and aromatherapy oils, and stimulate their tactile sense with suede cushions and touchy-feely sofa throws. Don't go over the top, though – fresh subtle scents from the garden are always better than overwhelming false fragrances.

While all this may sound a bit corny, and more like visiting a health farm than preparing your property for sale, remember that promoting your home as a happy, healthy environment will establish a sense of wellbeing and, more importantly, lead to a sale and a healthier bank balance. If you're selling your home because of unhappy circumstances, such as divorce or redundancy, you may be tempted to think that a problem shared is a problem halved – but *stop*! A new home should be a positive place: don't burden viewers with your tales of woe.

If your living room or master bedroom is south-facing, point this out to each prospective buyer. Wax lyrical about the light that floods in and sell this

▼ Enthuse about the benefits of your outside space and point out interesting views from each room to whet the appetite of potential buyers.

as a tangible benefit. If your home is north-facing and attracts less light play this down, but assure your viewers that as the sun moves around your home it warms up. If you can, try and arrange viewings when the natural light is at its best, to show your home at its most attractive.

When showing your property, maximize the impact by allowing viewers to enter small rooms first and then triumphantly leading them to the larger rooms to emphasize the space. Treat viewers as you would your friends and make them feel welcome. If you've looked after your property tell them about it: there's no point in keeping this vital information to yourself. If you've had the windows replaced, don't expect viewers to notice. Make an announcement. This will show that you care and that the property has been well maintained. It's a good idea to keep a record (before and after photographs, plans, colour schemes, etc.) of all the improvements you have made – a visible 'property MOT' that could make all the difference when the time comes to sell on.

The mechanics of selling

When someone takes a fancy to your home, they'll put in an offer. Now's the time to make your estate agent work for their money – you need to know who the purchasers are, what their financial situation is (i.e. have they got a mortgage sorted), how quickly they want to move and whether they've got to sell before buying. Think about what you want: a quick sale so you don't lose your dream property or as much money as possible. If you want to move quickly, be prepared to accept less than asking price, but set conditions. For instance, you agree not to show anyone round for the next three weeks, but the buyers must have their finance confirmed and a survey carried out by then; if they don't, you'll start remarketing. Remember, someone with cash at the ready and nowhere to sell could be a better bet than someone who promises more money, but hasn't yet found a buyer for their place.

If you've followed our advice, chances are you'll have swarms of people wanting to buy your home. If you get several offers, your estate agent might suggest going to sealed bids (see page 43). These secret bids have to be in by a certain date, then you decide which to accept. Sealed bids are stressful for buyers, but good news for vendors, because if people really want your house they may pay over the odds for it.

Once you've accepted an offer, instruct your solicitor to start the conveyancing process. They will apply for the title deeds to your home and draw up a contract to send to the buyer's solicitor. A surveyor will make an inspection and you'll be asked about your property's condition and any work you've had carried out. Few buyers happily take on major problems like subsidence, leaks or dodgy roofs so, if you know the survey will pick up something like this, either bite the bullet and pay for it to be fixed, or be prepared to drop your asking price. Don't cross your fingers and hope a surveyor won't notice that small patch of damp on the wall – they will.

What if you can't sell?

Even when the market's booming there are always properties that won't shift. If you haven't had much interest, make sure you're presenting your home in the best possible light. Ask your agent why things are slow, but don't be fobbed off with excuses about economic downturns or the importance of waiting for the 'right buyer'. The bottom line is, if your home isn't selling, it isn't priced right. If you've set an inflated asking price in the hope that you'll get a buyer eventually, your house could be on the market for months, which puts off potential buyers. So make sure you set a realistic figure.

Other ways to make money

If the prospect of buying, renovating and selling to make money sounds like hard work – and believe us it is – don't despair, because there are other ways to harvest an income through property. However, don't imagine that there are many get-rich-quick schemes to be had, as none of these options is without its disadvantages. *All* investments involve risks.

The rental market

More and more investors are now turning to the property rental market as a source of additional income. The growth of the housing industry and the poor performance of pension schemes has pushed many into planning for their own future by buying property as a long-term investment. The aim, of course, is for the rent you get to cover all your monthly repayments and to give you a profit on top. So you are looking for a steady monthly income as well as capital growth. An appreciating asset for the future and someone else paying for it into the bargain – sounds perfect, doesn't it?

▼ If you're kitting out your property for the rental market, choose a low-maintenance design that won't date.

So is it as easy as it sounds? In a word, *no*. Being a landlord is a huge responsibility and you will have to pay out for maintenance, insurance, management fees, council tax and mortgage repayments before the profits start to roll in. Add to that the cost of buying the property in the first place, doing it up and furnishing it, and you'll soon appreciate that this option is not for the lazy or faint-hearted. But that said, do your sums and if they make sense don't be put off. If you manage it properly renting out can be very lucrative indeed.

Buy-to-let schemes

Unless you earn enough to get a conventional second mortgage or have the cash to buy outright, a buy-to-let mortgage is the best way of financing an additional property. Devised by the Association of Residential Letting Agents (ARLA) and supported by the leading lending bodies, this particular type of mortgage is characterized by its low, highly competitive interest rates. Add to that the likelihood of sustained capital growth over the coming years and you'll soon see why there's been an explosion in the private rental sector.

People opt for rented accommodation for all sorts of reasons – they cannot afford to buy, they wish to stay mobile, they don't want the responsibilities of home-ownership, for example. And with house prices rising faster than the rate of inflation this group is getting bigger. So it's not surprising that there has been a concomitant growth in the number of people who have become landlords in the quest to service the demand. Until fairly recently, if you wanted to get a mortgage on a second property you would have been surcharged or forced to borrow at higher commercial rates. Furthermore, lenders would not have taken potential rental income into account when deciding how much money to give you. Buy-to-let schemes have put an end to all that.

There's little difference between buy-to-let and conventional mortgages, although most lenders will only lend up to 80% of the property's value. They may also insist an ARLA agent is appointed to manage the property.

Annual returns

As with all investments, performance is measured in profit, and the way to judge your performance is to measure the yearly rent as a proportion of the market value of the property. This will give you an annual yield figure. And don't think that only expensive properties are good for letting. In reality profits are often higher on smaller, cheaper homes. For most landlords the yield –

the rent received before deducting the costs of letting and management fees, maintenance and insurance – can be as high as 15%. The more expensive your property was to buy, the lower the yield will be, since the rent will make up a smaller propotion of its market value. However, the overall value of higher-priced homes can increase more in the long-term, so you won't be losing out.

It's also important when gauging potential returns to take into account the length of time a property could stay empty between lets – two or three months without a tenant will make a significant dent in your annual income. There can be many reasons for these gaps: the rent may be too high for the particular location or type of property, the accommodation may be in poor condition, or perhaps there is simply an oversupply in relation to demand.

To this end, and because there are no guarantees, it's important to tailor your property purchase to your prospective market in order to cut down on the likelihood of gaps in the tenancy. Think, and buy, laterally – for example, a furnished one-bedroom flat in the heart of a city would be ideal for a young professional and should work well, as should a three-bedroom unfurnished family home in an area with good schools.

Whatever the property type, it's important that it's well maintained, immaculately clean, secure, properly equipped and, if possible, serviced. That way you'll have a satisfied tenant, which should lead to a happy, hassle-free relationship for you all. And, of course, a longer rental. To maintain the value of your investment you also need to make sure the tenants look after the property so, even if you're only renting the property out for a few months, always draw up a contract, check references and insist the place is well maintained.

And remember – the real profit is often not the monthly rental but the resale value accruing in your property – a valuable asset for the future paid for by your tenants.

Letting agents

For trouble-free letting it's worth considering employing an agent. A good letting agent will advertise your property, arrange viewings, vet prospective tenants, check their references and draw up a standard contract. For an additional fee they will aslo manage things for you, collect rent and deal with cleaning and maintenance. This is worthwhile if you live far away or are too busy to deal with problems yourself, but you'll pay dearly for the service – sometimes up to 15% of the monthly rent (make sure you factor in this charge when you're calculating your potential profit). Choose agents belonging to the ARLA or the National Approved Letting Scheme (NALS), because they have to adhere to certain standards.

Holiday homes

Turning a second property into a holiday home is another way of making money, though it calls for a specialist approach if you are to make that all-important profit. Again the crucial consideration is to tailor your home to an existing market – after all, there's no point in buying something on an island with no power, no transportation links and no services. Mass appeal is what you're after, so think a thatched cottage or a converted barn in the Cotswolds, an old fisherman's house overlooking the sea in Cornwall or something within range of a tourist hot spot like Stratford-upon-Avon, York or Edinburgh.

Before you invest it's wise to talk to holiday-cottage rental companies to check your potential property meets their criteria. Remember that standards should be extremely high as you're offering a comfortable holiday retreat. This means your property should be well furnished, well equipped and immaculate, with controllable heating and hot water. The better it is, the more likely that your guests will spread the word. Holiday companies do charge for their services, and no holiday home is guaranteed full occupancy for 52 weeks a year, so take this into account when working out profitability. As with the private rental sector, often it is not the monthly income that will make you rich but the appreciation of your holiday home as a capital asset.

Renting while renovating

You might be able to rent out a spare room while doing your place up to help with costs. If a property is your sole residence you won't incur any tax liability,

▲ If you're buying to rent to the holiday market, select property with a specific appeal, to ensure maximum return on your investment.

provided the amount you earn in a year from rent doesn't exceed £4250, which works out at just over £350 a month. This is known as the Rent-a-Room scheme. Be realistic about what you charge if you're doing major renovation work – most lodgers won't want to eat supper by candlelight while you re-route electric cables or to doze off to a background noise of drilling.

If you earn more than £4250 a year in rent, you'll have to pay tax on the extra. Similarly, if you're renting out a property and not living there yourself, it won't come under the Rent-a-Room scheme and you'll be taxed. In this case you can claim expenses for things like utitility bills, insurance premiums, water rates and maintenance and repair costs; if you've got someone paying to lodge in your home, you can't claim these expenses. Finally, remember that if you've rented out your home other than through the Rent-a-Room scheme, you may have to pay Capital Gains Tax when you come to sell it.

Location fees

If your home is significantly individual, has traditional period features or is otherwise noteworthy in any way it might be suitable as a location for a film. Unless you own a palace or a stately home you will never be able to rely on film companies to provide you with a steady income, but it can be fun to be involved in filming – and a nice little wedge of cash is always useful.

We once rented out the dining room in our Glasgow apartment to an advertising agency. They arrived at 8 a.m., filmed a television commercial and left at 1 p.m., cleaning up as they went and leaving everything exactly as it had been (they took Polaroids to guide them) when they arrived. We got an insight into how commercials are made and got paid £1000 for the privilege. Not a bad morning's work!

If you want to register your property look in the phone book for film and TV location agents or video production companies, or get in touch with your local TV station.

Conclusion

So there you have it – the essential Justin-and-Colin guide to property profiteering. In a market that can move up as quickly as it can fall down, our final word of advice would be: CAUTION – exercise it at all times. But if you enjoy the property market one-tenth as much as we do, then the fun that lies ahead will be immeasurable, in spite of the risks. This book should provide you with all the help you need. Good luck and happy house-hunting!

Leadhall Way, ROSSET GREEN, HARROGATE

Property profile

A two-reception, four-bedroom detached property set in overgrown grounds, with generous proportions, but with old and outdated central heating, kitchen units from the ark, drab décor and in drastic need of renewal. Full rewiring and replumbing required. Offers around £255,000. Freehold.

The house had great potential but little else going for it and we jumped in with a lower bid of £236,000, fully expecting it to be rejected so we would have to reoffer and meet somewhere in the middle. But surprise, surprise! Our offer was acceptable to the vendors and we took possession some 12 weeks later. Here are our sums:

Buying price:	£236,000
Buying costs:	£4000
Development costs:	£90,000
Selling costs:	£4000
Selling price:	£335,000
Profit:	£1000

Whoever coined the phrase 'it's grim up north' clearly never witnessed Harrogate in North Yorkshire. Visiting this town for the first time, while isolating property 'hot spots', we found that it's actually one of Britain's best kept secrets. Think beautiful Victorian squares and cosy traditional restaurants, but then add a smattering of cosmopolitan shopping and cool, bustling bars with state-of-the-art design, and you should start to get the picture. But there's more – this bustling town is also neatly wrapped up in some of the most beautiful and sprawling countryside Yorkshire has to offer.

Location

Harrogate is a rising star in Britain's relocation league due to its proximity to three of the country's leading universities – Leeds, Bradford and York – its thriving business community and its excellent transportation infrastructure. We both agreed that where there's relocation, there is also likely to be a buoyant housing market.

Our gut instincts told us that this area would have colossal appeal. Sizing up the market via numerous trips around local estate agents revealed a mixed housing stock ranging from new-build homes, barn conversions and Victorian villas to modern urban-style penthouse apartments. Importantly, demand seemed to outstrip supply and we both felt very positive.

Why Rossett Green?

After viewing a recently constructed family home priced at £430,000 we chanced upon a similarly sized but much older one in Rossett

Green. When competing with new developments you have to outline every advantage to make sure that what you're selling is as attractive as possible. The main plus point with this house was its perfect situation – in an established residential pocket on the south side of the town where prices are usually high because of easy access to road networks and excellent local schooling. Here we also had ideal 'redefinition' prospects – a boring house with potential, in a popular area.

Suffering from tiredness (the house, not us!), it was competitively priced at £255,000 due to the fact it had gone largely unchanged since its construction in the late 1950s. But who, specifically, in Harrogate should the property be aimed at? To be as well informed as possible about our target market, we spent time in the area looking at who was buying and selling, who was renovating and what they were doing both internally and externally. We came to the conclusion that in the leafy culs-de-sac of Rossett Green late-30-something couples, possibly with young families, should be our goal.

Our plans

The challenge here was to rebrand a dated property and make it more attractive – and therefore much more desirable – than its contemporaries. Externally, the 1950s windows and boxy house style were dated and needed

FIRST FLOOR before

FIRST FLOOR after

◀ Adding rooms adds value – the new conservatory not only enhanced the open-plan living area but it also increased the saleability of the property.

GROUND FLOOR before

GROUND FLOOR after

immediate attention. Internally, the prevailing feel was decoratively challenged to say the very least! The house simply required a brand-new identity – one that would fit more accurately with the expectations of today's very demanding and discerning home-buyer.

We set about planning how the available space should be used to accommodate a modern family. This house represented the perfect challenge for us: accustomed as we were to creating gorgeous living spaces for cool urbanites, we had less experience in tailoring a home specifically for the family market. But hey – we have always loved an experience-developing challenge. We decided to extend the main family bathroom, add an en suite to one of the larger bedrooms and give the boxy downstairs rooms a more modern open-plan feel.

With current interior trends favouring the return of the kitchen as the heart of the home we planned to concentrate our main efforts there and open up the space to create a unified dining, living and eating zone. The identity of the area would shift from cold compartmentalized solitude to free-flowing shared family space, which definitely made this an easier prospect for the market. The addition of a smart new conservatory would complete the sleek modern look. Ambitious plans, we agree, and the costs soon began to spiral.

Outside

The dated appearance of the outside of the property offered us a unique opportunity to indulge in a little exterior make-over. We decided to replace the windows with faux Georgian double-glazed units and alter the shape of the upper centre window from plain boring square to architecturally pleasing circle.

The next task in hand was to alter the boxy appearance of the bay window in the lounge by redesigning the flat roof with a tiled pitch, which we extended to overhang the front door and form a porch. While we were at it, we replaced the front door with a matching white Georgian-style alternative which effectively completed the picture.

Next, we replaced the dated green garage-door with a white panelled one that provided an instant lift. A front garden tidy-up, a ton of gravel and some smart new gates gave buyers a taste of what lay ahead. Although the changes we made were fairly simple, they radically redefined the exterior (see page 136).

The rear exterior

To make the most of the valuable space at the rear of the property and to develop the concept of the modern family home further, we extended the dining area into an attractive conservatory, with an external raised boardwalk leading to a new door that connected to the breakfast area at the far end of the kitchen (see page 117). Doing this added valuable suntrap seating (good old British weather permitting, of course) and stopped the rear of the property being so incredibly bland. Beauty and functionality – what could be a better mix in saleability terms? We also returfed the garden, repaired the greenhouse and made general horticultural tweaks to provide impact.

The living room

'Lounge' is now simply one of the things we do in our living rooms, so we opted for easy-maintenance furnishings and a predominantly neutral scheme that would allow a host of

▶ Replacing a tired fireplace with a cutting-edge alternative catapults the room into the twenty-first century.

possible uses for this open-plan room. With its low-key, soft blue paintwork and the carpeting, the room was perfect for relaxing, reading, eating, snuggling up or entertaining. Updating here meant out with the 1950s tiled fireplace and in with something considerably more modern. We opted for a 'CVO Firebowl' – form and function entwined, it is as beautiful switched off as it is switched on. Opening up the back of the fire space was a low-cost, high-style way of giving two interconnecting rooms a welcome style boost, and provided a stylish visual link between both zones – an important consideration when creating open-plan living (see above).

The dining room

Room for dining was limited in the original configuration so we placed our table next to the conservatory, which is semi-open-plan to the dining and kitchen space, creating an area of flexible and generous space. This clean, neutral area is now perfectly sited to serve the living room and the kitchen. When it came to dressing the space, we treated the conservatory and dining room as one and laid the conservatory out with after-dinner seating (see page 56).

Kitchen

The emphasis here was on structural change. The kitchen was small and gloomy, so first, having consulted a structural engineer, we knocked down the wall of built-in cupboards between it and the dining room. Then we borrowed space by losing the rear downstairs loo and the boiler room at the opposite end and building up the floor in the space that remained. A modern combi-boiler housed in the garage replaced the cumbersome old one and still left space for a slick new tiled WC. The kitchen is now centrally placed between the garden and the dining room, ideal for the summer months when the decked rear patio will become the focus for dining.

We decided to give the kitchen a fairly modern look and opted for white units with black worktops. Relying on the fittings for design attraction, we steered away from painted walls and instead coloured the room with

▶ Sometimes less can be more. Only a change in décor was needed to bring this room to life.

luxurious limestone flooring, steel blinds and a chrome radiator (see page 81).

The hall and stairway

Good advice is never to overlook the hall – after all, it's the first space potential buyers view and a great spot to make a first impression. To show off our new round hall-window we removed the closed banister on the stairs and replaced it with an open square-spindled one – this not only looked more attractive but also allowed light from above to filter downstairs. Carpeting was by way of a neutral stair runner complete with chrome stair-rods, while three frosted glass light fittings, hung at different heights in a cluster, completed the simple yet gorgeous look (see page 92).

Bedrooms one, two and three

Space speaks for itself, but just to be sure we dressed the larger two bedrooms with double beds, wardrobes and chairs to allow potential buyers to get a feel for the square footage (see

above and page 143 left). They were initially neutrally decorated, but we acted on estate agent advice and later decided to add splashes of colour in the form of accent walls.

The accent of the smaller bedroom was in the form of a striped paint effect, replicated on a 'stretch' canvas to create a complementary artwork (see page 143 right). The young feel of this room made it the perfect hideaway for kids but could appeal to teenagers too. Remember – it's important to create spaces in your home that are as flexible as possible. That way potential buyers will never be stuck for choice.

Bedroom four

We decided to give this bedroom a Laura Ashley look with a golden bed, Regency-striped wallpaper and luxurious linens. Opening up a doorway into the previously landing-accessed WC gave us more space and allowed us to create a stunning en suite, complete with Victorian-style brickwork tiles and border. White sanitarywares and Amtico flooring made a simple statement.

The bathroom

We decided to knock the bathroom through to the commodious water-tank cupboard beyond (we moved the tank into the attic) to provide ourselves with loads of extra space for a family-sized bathroom. Walnut panelling, a white suite and frosted glass panels were chosen to underpin a modern scheme that is half hotel-boutique chic and half friendly, family values. Who could resist?

Estate agency time

When the house was ready, we invited local estate agents to cast their eye around. Each expert said pretty much the same thing – they pronounced it one of the most beautiful homes to grace the local market and assured us it would be easy to sell. Inspired by their enthusiasm we made a mistake – one that we, with all our experience, should never have made. We became greedy. Originally we had agreed that £370,000 would be an acceptable price, but all that fell by the wayside as the agents suggested we could achieve nearer £400,000.

So what eventually happened? Well, the price was just too high. For fear of sending ourselves to hell and back by recounting the full tale, we'll fill you in, briefly, on the salient points:

- On the advice of our agent, we conducted an 'open day', with drinks and canapés, to show the house to as many people as possible. The resulting melee and volume of apparent interest intimidated genuine potential buyers. We remember one couple who said they'd love to buy the property, but were convinced its sale would go to sealed bids.
- During the very early stages of marketing we turned down an offer for £380,000, certain that we would be able to achieve a higher figure.

- By chipping away at our guide price over the next few months we created a 'property stigma' that proved well nigh impossible to shift. The price was slashed time and time again until most potential buyers lost faith.
- The house was just not family-friendly enough, with a fireplace open on two sides, an unprotected hob and an entirely open-plan ground floor.

Desperate to escape Harrogate, we redecorated in an attempt to broaden appeal, added more storage units in the kitchen, as well as a tiled splashback between the hob and the dining area to make the kitchen more child-friendly, and changed agents several times. After an agonizing eight months, an offer arrived for £335,000. With a profit of just £1000, we crawled away to lick our wounds. Still, at least we hadn't made a loss and we learnt a great deal from the painful experience – the emotional scars are still with us.

At the time of going to press ...

- Property 5 – a dated four-bedroomed town house in Leamington Spa needing extensive renovation. Bought for £358,000, we've just received an offer of £510,000 and hope to make a profit of £30,000.
- Property 6 – a run-down semi-detached villa in Edinburgh with 6 bedrooms, bought for £485,000. Riddled with dry rot, the house took 15 weeks to renovate. We sold it for £807,000, giving us a healthy profit of £107,000.
- Property 7 – a two-bedroomed property in Belgravia, London, bought for £780,500 (awaiting completion). We plan to refurbish and extend the house, in order to sell for £1,000,000.

Glossary

APR – annual percentage rate; total actual cost to you of the loan per year

Arrangement fee – amount charged by lender to set up your mortgage

Broker – someone who finds suitable mortgages, loans and other financial services

Building insurance – insurance that covers structural damage to your property

Buildings survey – detailed report about the property you intend to buy; also called a full structural survey

Capital – total sum borrowed in the form of a mortgage

Chain – most property transactions happen within a chain, whereby A buys from B, who buys from C, who buys from D. At the lower end of the chain there may be a first-time buyer, and the people at the top end may be moving abroad or going into rented accommodation.

Completion – the point where contracts are exchanged and ownership of the property legally passes to the buyer

Contents insurance – covers any loss or damage to possessions contained within your home

Contract – legal document needed to transfer ownership of a property

Conveyancing – legal work involved in buying and selling a property

Deeds (or title deeds) – show the rightful owner of the property and are transferred to the purchaser when a sale is completed; often held by the mortgage lender

Deposit – money put down by the purchaser at the time of exchange

Disbursements – expenses paid by the solicitor on behalf of the purchaser, which are later added to the bill

Exchange of contracts – the point at which the buyer and seller transfer legal documents associated with the sale and are bound to the deal

Fixtures and fittings list – complete list of everything included in a sale, such as curtains and carpets

Freehold – outright ownership of a property and the land it stands on

Gazumping – the seller, having already accepted an offer, accepts a higher one from another buyer

Gazundering – the buyer forces the seller to accept a lower offer for a property just before contracts are due to be exchanged, usually by threatening to pull out of the deal

Home buyer's survey – more detailed survey than a valuation report, to look for potential structural problems in a property

Land registry – agency with which all properties and their owners are registered

Lease – legal document by which the owner of a freehold property lets out premises for a specific time and at a certain price

Leasehold – ownership of the lease

Local authority search – investigation carried out by a solicitor to make sure nothing is being proposed that affects the property you want to buy

Redemption – when a mortgage is fully repaid

Retention – part of a mortgage loan that is held back until certain repairs are carried out

Stamp duty – government tax on the purchase of a house, based on its price and ranging from 1% to 4% for properties over £59,999

Structural survey – report carried out by a surveyor to make sure a property is structurally sound and listing any work that needs to be done

Term – period over which a mortgage is spread

Title – the legal right to ownership of a property

Valuation report – carried out by the lender to ensure the property is worth as much or more than the amount of the proposed loan

Useful information

Start your search for a new property here – these websites and societies are often our first port of call:

Property websites
www.heritage.co.uk
(specialist agent handling listed property)
www.home.co.uk
www.hometrack.co.uk
(for information on market trends)
www.hotproperty.co.uk
www.primelocation.com
www.propertylive.co.uk
(part of the NAEA website)
www.propertypresentation.co.uk
www.rightmove.co.uk
www.thepropertyguide.co.uk
www.upmystreet.co.uk

For average UK house prices
www.landreg.gov.uk
tel: 020 7917 8888
www.nationwide.co.uk
www.hbosplc.com
(The Halifax) tel: 01422 333333

Estate agents
www.naea.co.uk (National Association of Estate Agents)
www.oea.co.uk (Ombudsman Scheme for Estate Agents)

Flood warnings
To discover if a postcode is in a potential flood district, contact www.environment-agency.gov.uk

Other useful sites
www.savebritainsheritage.org
tel: 020 7253 3500
www.countrylife.co.uk
www.rics.org
(Royal Institute of Chartered Surveyors)

Scotland
www.espc.co.uk
(Edinburgh Solicitors Property Centre)

Here is a selection of our favourite suppliers:

Alternative Flooring Company (carpets and flooring)
www.alternative-flooring.co.uk
Tel: 01264 335111

The Amtico Company (flooring)
www.amtico.com
Tel: 0800 667766

And So To Bed (beds)
www.andsotobed.co.uk
Tel: 0808 144 4343

Bo Concept (furniture)
www.boconcept.com
Tel: 0141 204 3441

Bute Fabrics Ltd (curtains)
www.butefabrics.com
Tel: 01700 503734

Cannock Gates Ltd (gates and garden furniture)
www.cannockgates.co.uk
Tel: 01543 462500

Crown Trade Paint (paint)
www.crowntrade.co.uk
Tel: 01254 704951

Ducal (furniture)
www.ducal.com

Dulux (paint)
www.dulux.co.uk
Tel: 01753 550555

Fired Earth (flooring and paint)
www.firedearth.co.uk
Tel: 020 7589 0489

Gazco (gas fires)
www.gazco.com
Tel: 01392 474061

Georgian Antiques (fine furniture)
www.georgianantiques.net
Tel: 0131 553 7286

Habitat (furniture)
www.habitat.co.uk

Hillary's Blinds (blinds)
www.hillarys.co.uk
Tel: 0800 587 6469

House of Fraser (accessories)
www.houseoffraser.co.uk
Tel: 020 7963 2000

Ikea Ltd (accessories and furniture)
www.ikea.co.uk
Tel: 0845 355 1141

Ideal Standard (bathrooms)
www.ideal-standard.co.uk
Tel: 01482 346 461

Laura Ashley (furniture)
www.lauraashley.com
Tel: 08705 622 116

Lee Longlands (furniture)
www.leelonglands.co.uk
Tel: 0121 643 9101

Maravilla (bedroom furniture)
www.maravilla.co.uk
Tel: 0117 974 4949

Marks & Spencer (furniture)
www.marksandspencer.com
Tel: 020 7268 1234

MFI (bathrooms, bedrooms and kitchens)
www.mfi.co.uk
Tel: 0870 607 5093

MK Electric (light switches)
www.mkelectric.co.uk
Tel: 0870 240 3385

Myson (radiators)
www.myson.co.uk
Tel: 0191 491 7530

Percy Whale (fine furniture)
www.percywhale.co.uk
Tel: 01926 421288

Plan It Earth (flooring and wall tiles)
www.plan-it-earth.co.uk
Tel: 01943 831300

Porcelanosa (bathroom tiles)
www.porcelanosa.co.uk
Tel: 0800 915 4000

Precious Stone (worktops)
Tel: 01422 246863

Rangemaster (cookers)
www.rangemaster.co.uk
Tel: 0870 789 5107

Selfridges (accessories)
www.selfridges.co.uk
Tel: 08708 377 377

Sofa Workshop (furniture)
www.sofaworkshop.co.uk
Tel: 01798 343 400

The Velux Company Ltd (skylight windows)
www.velux.co.uk
Tel: 0800 316882

Viva Sofa (furniture)
www.vivasofa.co.uk
Tel: 01443 239 444

Vogue Furniture (furniture)
Tel: 0141 764 1144

Index